T0118266

STIFF
THEM!

STIFF THEM!

Your Guide to Paying Zero Dollars to the IRS, Student Loans, Credit Cards, Medical Bills, and More

Dr. Gary S. Goodman

MEDIA

Published 2018 by Gildan Media LLC
aka G&D Media
www.GandDmedia.com

STIFF THEM!. Copyright © 2018 by Dr. Gary S. Goodman. All rights reserved.

Printed in the United States of America. No part of this book may be reproduced or transmitted in any form, by any means, (electronic, photocopying, recording, or otherwise) without the prior written permission of the author. No liability is assumed with respect to the use of the information contained within. Although every precaution has been taken, the author and publisher assume no liability for errors or omissions. Neither is any liability assumed for damages resulting from the use of the information contained herein. This book is not a legal or a CPA book and it does not offer legal or accounting advice. You need to ask your personal lawyer and personal CPA before using the recommendations included in the book to assure they address your specific circumstances and meet current legal and agency requirements.

FIRST EDITION 2018

Front Cover design by David Rheinhardt of Pyrographx

Interior design by Meghan Day Healey of Story Horse, LLC

Library of Congress Cataloging-in-Publication Data is available upon request

ISBN: 978-1-7225-0036-8

10   9   8   7   6   5   4   3   2   1

Contents

Introduction and Preview

Sure, in a perfect world you want to do the right thing and meet every single obligation.

Don't we all?

But when it comes to paying back exorbitant amounts of debt, being virtuous in this way is too expensive, and most of us simply can't afford it.

There is a reason you and tens of millions of others are buried in debt. Today's world is set up so most of us will fail financially.

We're enticed to purchase what we don't need, to accept and use credit cards we can't pay, and to rack up student loans that lead to knowledge that is not in demand and to jobs that don't exist.

Forty-four percent of Americans are underemployed, which means you are overqualified by virtue of experience or education and you are underpaid. Where are you going to find the money to get the necessities of life, let alone retire IRS debts, student loans, usurious credit cards, subprime car loans, and other obligations?

Your health-care plan probably isn't a genuine health plan, but an illusion, a trap with a huge deductible and big premiums. From personal experience, I can tell you that one trip to the emergency room, without an overnight stay or even an ocean view, can run up a tab of $18,000 for a kidney stone that passes from your body without surgery, or for any medicinal intervention.

Should you stay awake at night sweating over failing to pay a bill like that? And if you choose to suffer guilt or remorse, what good does it do?

You don't get extra points for berating yourself or being distracted from the other significant aspects of your life.

What options do you have? Fortunately, there is a remedy, expressed in this two-word marching order:

STIFF THEM!

Pay less, or pay nothing, but know this: you don't have to pay "as agreed."

The outfits that are badgering folks like you for payment are in business to withstand losses.

They have already priced into the cost of their goods and services the amount you owe and more, in the expectation that they will *not* get paid by a significant number of people.

Take the IRS, the largest collection agency in the world. Will the IRS shut its doors if you don't pay in full the demand they sent you? If the government runs short of funds, it will print more money, one way or another. Plus, there are billionaires that don't pay a penny in tax.

But as you can imagine, there is an art and a science to untangling the debts and other financial tentacles that are squeezing the joy and life from you.

I'm going to teach you two things: First, how to repay these entities supercheaply, if you feel you must. So you'll be significantly or at least partly stiffing them rather than totally and utterly stiffing them.

This is the "pay-pennies-on-the-dollar" approach to debt settlement.

Second, I'll show you how to escape repayment completely, if your circumstances require it, if your hardships are so great, or if you are simply ornery or a complete flake and you don't want to pay a penny.

I have been in the business of tax resolution, credit-card and medical-debt resolution, student-loan consolidations, and collections, and I have consulted for major financial companies, such as Discover Card.

I know how the IRS works and the many ways you can pay less in taxes, or pay nothing at all—completely legal ways, mind you. I have helped hundreds of people to pay back zero or tiny amounts to resolve millions of dollars of debt. I have helped graduates and dropouts to escape from student-loan hell, in many cases to pay zero dollars per month with total debt forgiveness after a stated term of years.

I teach best practices in negotiation at the two highest-rated universities in the United States, and I am a licensed attorney. I know the ins and outs of bankruptcy.

We'll dedicate an entire section to probing the tyranny of the FICO score and show how to beat the credit bureaus.

I had a brilliant professor in college, who issued this advice to those of us that were studying economics: "Borrow heavily when you're young, because you'll be paying it back in cheaper dollars."

He was right. Inflation made the student loans I took out far cheaper by the time I had to repay them.

But I have that teacher beaten when it comes to advice. I say, "Borrow heavily at any age, because you can very possibly pay back in ZERO dollars!"

Why am I sharing these insider tips with you? Certainly I like writing, and I want to sell a few books.

But I'm really a David-versus-Goliath kind of guy. As my dad put it, "In our family, we always root for the underdog."

That's my thing. The IRS, the big banks, the medical-industrial complex, and others have plenty of clout and money, and they're used to getting their way. If I can put a pebble or two into your slingshot to lower their odds of beating you into submission, then it's my pleasure to do so.

In the material that follows, you'll notice many counterintuitive insights that will change the playing field to your advantage.

Chapter-by-Chapter Preview

Lots of books tout the virtues of becoming debt-free. To me, that's a little too simple-minded. As you'll soon see, there are two kinds of debt: good and bad. You'll learn about them in chapter 1. Obviously, you should consider each one in a different light. Bad debt is probably what you're saddled with today, so we'll invest a lot of time talking about minimizing it and zeroing it out. But good debt is an entirely different breed. What are the differences?

They say you don't get what you deserve in life: you get what you're able to negotiate. This is especially true with credit-card debt resolution. In chapter 2 we're going to explore the essentials of exploiting your bargaining power. And when it comes to debt elimination, you have plenty of power. You may not feel that way at this moment, but at the end of this chapter you'll probably have a change of heart. Everything is negotiable!

Chapter 3 sings the praises of bankruptcy as a means of zeroing out your debts and getting a fresh start. As a rule, bankruptcy gets a bad rap, especially from creditors. There's a good reason that they recoil, like Dracula seeing the dawn streaking through the window: their right to collect from you will turn to ashes when you file for Chapter 7. You'll learn how this is different than Chapter 13, and you'll develop insights into bankruptcy as a possible remedy for your debt troubles and as a platform for quickly rebuilding your creditworthiness.

We all know that there are two immutable forces in life: death and taxes. I'll show you that this notion is only half-true. In chapter 4, you'll learn how to stiff the IRS, legally, of course. There is a vital difference between *tax avoidance*, which the legendary judge Learned Hand said is every American's right, and *tax evasion*, which is what they nailed gangster Al Capone for, providing him with the glorious opportunity to die in prison. This book isn't about seizing every available deduction (though there are notably fewer since the recent changes made in the tax code by the U.S. Congress). It is about reducing or eliminating tax debt after you have incurred it and have been billed for it by the IRS.

In chapter 5, we'll turn our attention to student-loan forgiveness—how to pay fewer or even zero dollars on your educational debts. You'll learn how student-loan debt exceeds credit-card debt. It is a burden being borne by more than 40 million people. Chances are very good that you have graduated and are underemployed. This means you are laboring in a job beneath your training and experience. And if this is the case, you're being paid far less than you imagined receiving when you took out your student loans. We'll talk about qualifying for deferred and reduced monthly outlays, which may amount to zero dollars per month, depending on your income.

Managing your debts and pursuing any of the remedies provided in this book is not a simple matter of "do this and then do that." Of course, there are some procedures that need to be followed, as I've indicated. But addressing your debts and resolving to resolve them takes a decision on your part.

Equally important, in chapter 6 we explore a crucial question: why try to pay off your bills? Debtors can waste time and resources throwing good money after bad. They make minimum payments for years and years without denting the overall size of their credit-card debts. This makes banks happy, because they maximize their interest earnings. But it robs debtors of the ability to invest their modest resources elsewhere. You'll see how if you're exerting superhuman effort in most endeavors, including debt resolution, you're probably doing something terribly wrong. If you ask most people what they regret about making crucial decisions regarding their finances, especially filing for bankruptcy, they won't say they should not have done it. They ask, "Why didn't I do it sooner?"

Chapter 7 will help you to restore your financial self-confidence. Once you have decided to take action, you'll need to recover your monetary self-esteem and mojo. You've taken a hit and cut your losses, and now you need to climb back into the saddle. You'll accomplish this partly by making better financial choices. You'll see that going through hardships and suffering losses is part of the trajectory of the rich and famous. You'll understand that your excesses weren't caused merely from wrongful spending. They were the result of wrongful lending, as well. Punctuating your financial experiences properly, putting them into the most sympathetic perspective, will enable you to focus on getting good credit instead of bad, and accumulating wealth instead of useless debts.

You're going to like what's ahead. These insights and immediately practical tips will help you to take back the power that we needlessly yield to these petty tyrants—creditors—and place that power squarely in your hands, where it belongs.

Chapter 1

Good Debt and Bad Debt

Most of us think we know what debt is all about. All we have to do is check out the bills we receive and our credit-card balances.

We borrowed, and we owe more than we borrowed because of interest charges. So we have to pay it back.

What else is there to know?

A lot, as it turns out. When I was in college, I bought a book with an odd, counterintuitive title:

How to Borrow Your Way to a Great Fortune.

The author, Tyler Hicks, sang the praises of OPM, which stands for Other People's Money. His thesis is if you can put other people's money to better use than they can, then borrow it.

Pay them interest, of course, which they'll be happy to view as the highest and best use of their funds. But you'll know better, because you'll be bringing in a much better return on their money than they are receiving.

This may seem abstract, but it isn't. It is the age-old capitalistic concept of buying low and selling high. In this case you're buying, or, if you like, renting money.

And then you're reselling the same money you have been loaned, but at a higher rate.

Technically and quite practically, you're going into debt for the purpose of turning a profit, or in some cases with the idea of building long-term wealth.

Seen this way, incurring debt is not only OK and not to be avoided, but it is something to purposely acquire, because if you use it in the right way, debt becomes an asset.

Just as you need steel, plastic, and increasingly today aluminum, to build cars, you need debt—and the more the merrier—to create wealth. That's what Hicks is saying.

This is *good debt*. Debt that puts you in a better position tomorrow than you're in today is actually positive.

If there's good debt, there must be the other kind, correct? Yes, it is *bad debt*. And we'll get to that in a minute.

But let's start with an example. If you buy a house, as a general rule you are taking on good debt. Why is this? As you know, homes usually appreciate in value.

They'll sell for more in the future than they do today. And despite tax reform, which has limited the amount you can write off of your property taxes, there are still advantages to home ownership.

For one thing, as long as you pay your mortgage, taxes, and insurance, and the state doesn't forcibly buy your home to blow it up for a new highway, you can live there, uninterrupted, for the remainder of your days. That confers serenity, which is an antidote to the other stresses of modern life.

This peace of mind and ability to plan where you will be in the long term delivers "psychic income." You can't cash it in at the bank, but it is meaningful.

If you contrast it with the insecurity renters can feel, being subject to big price increases and the whims of owners, who can sell your home out from under you, there is much to be said for home ownership, if only because of the feeling of control it confers.

Of course, one of the downsides of stiffing them—walking away from your bills—is that it can make qualifying for a home loan later on more difficult. However, there are various workarounds.

You can get owner financing, if the people that are selling have the deed to the place and are willing to carry back all or part of the mortgage amount. This is a smart strategy even if you have sterling credit, because you can avoid paying high loan fees to conventional mortgage lenders.

Of course, even with bad credit, if your down payment is sufficient, you can find lenders that are willing to take the risk. They know that in case they have to foreclose, they will receive their entire investment back.

I'm getting afield here. Suffice it to say that home ownership is mostly a good idea, and the debt it requires you to take on is good debt. It positions you well for the future, because it is an appreciating asset.

In *How to Borrow Your Way to a Great Fortune*, Tyler Hicks recommends buying a lot of houses and renting them out. If your rents cover your expenses, you're in good shape. And he is very high on the idea of getting owner financing.

The key to real-estate investing is leverage. Basically this means that the less you need to put down in cash to buy a property, the better your gains will be.

Let's say you purchase a home for $400,000, and it appreciates in value by 3% per year on average. After you've owned it for a year, it is valued at $412,000. On paper, you have "made" a gain of $12,000.

If you made an initial down payment of $80,000, your "return" on that investment is NOT $80,000 times 3%. That would be $2400. A decent stock could pay you that amount in dividends.

Your return is actually 3% times $400,000, or, as I said before, $12,000. You've made a nifty 15% return on your $80,000 down-payment money in a single year.

Let's say, instead of $80,000, which is 20% of the purchase price, you could buy for only 10% down, that is, by investing only $40,000. Then that $12,000 gain would represent an astonishing return of 30% to you.

That's just year one. Through what is often called "the miracle of compounding," your home, now valued at $412,000 will appreciate by 3% in year number two. That means it will increase by $12,360, and will be worth $424,360.

If you put down $40,000, you will have already realized a payback of 60.9% of it after 24 months. After your year three, the home will be valued at $437,090.

By that time, your payback on your down payment will be almost complete: you'll be looking at a return of 92.7% of what you originally put in.

The miracle is that your 90% of debt on the property is earning you money at *compounding* rates of return, while you are repaying your mortgage at *simple interest*— while you are mowing the lawn and eating breakfast and sleeping soundly at night.

This isn't just good debt, it's GREAT debt!

I should point out that if you sold your home after one year, using a realtor, your gain would probably be eaten up by his or her fees, which typically run 5%. But you're not going to cash out that soon.

Plus, you can always take a short course and get your own real-estate sales license. This could be used to negotiate a split of commissions with the listing realtor. I've done this, and I currently have a California broker's license, entitling me to a bigger slice of the pie.

Once more, good debt positions you for a better future. Bad debt does the opposite. It mires you in the past, paying for trifles that depreciate in value or have been completely consumed.

Buying clothing on a department store's credit card is an example of bad debt. Typically clothes are fashion items, designed to become obsolete after a season or two. They are poorly made and wear out easily. And they cost too much.

Now on top of these faults, you're borrowing to finance these flimsies. That's just all kinds of stupid. Over time, my philosophy has become, "Better to wear it out than to throw it out!"

When we were playing tennis the other day, my wife noticed my shirt was becoming more holes than shirt, so we tossed that one away at the park. I kid you not. I've extended the life of so many things that when I do buy a half-dozen new socks, as I did yesterday, it's time to break out the champagne!

I would also classify some student-loan debts as good ones. You might expect a guy with five earned degrees to say as much, but I mean it. As Plato reportedly said, "Education is the one good thing we can't get too much of," and I agree with him.

But there are smart ways to take on student-loan debt.

For example, as a general rule, federally insured student loans are not dischargeable in bankruptcy, with a few exceptions that I cover in another section. But as I write this, I can tell you many PRIVATE student loans *can* be wiped in a Chapter 7 liquidation case.

That is something to remember if you believe there are three immutable forces, death, taxes, and student-loan repayments!

I have to say you need to attend an accredited institution of higher learning or a trade school that has a solid track record of placing its graduates in paying jobs.

Don't kid yourself that a buy-your-degree-mill that is in the printing business and not in the education field will do anything for you except take your dough and put you into debt.

I appeared on the same dais as a prominent speaker and up-and-coming author. He called himself Dr. So and So, and he referred to himself that way throughout his talk.

We got to know each other, and I had a client who was seeking another speaker for an annual sales meeting. I thought this fellow would be perfect. But that "doctor" title didn't quite seem right. Dynamic as he was in speaking to audiences, he didn't strike me as the type that would really develop new knowledge, as legitimate PhDs like me are trained to do.

So before putting his name into play for the occasion, I looked up the school that granted his doctorate. Actually, I asked the research librarian at the University of Southern California, from which I graduated, to do it for me.

He reported that it was a diploma mill. If you paid enough money, you could use your life experiences as substitutes for attending classes. And you could tender a simple research paper and call it your "doctoral dissertation."

Long story short, my new pal was a phony. Well, at least his degree and his claim to being an intellectual were fraudulent.

I called him and urged him to drop the "doctor" title. "You don't need it," I said.

He did exactly that. He was a smash hit at my client's event, and this same fellow went on to become a coeditor of one of the best selling self-help books of all time.

His phony degree was a time bomb. Sooner or later, he would have been unmasked as an impostor.

Don't go into debt to get that kind of pretend education.

That said, there are some other things to avoid. Paying out-of-state tuition, which is about the same as private university prices, is dumb. If you're going to attend a state school, go to your own.

Also, community colleges can be a tremendous bargain for the first two years, even at today's prices. When I went, I paid the grand sum of $7.50 to take up to 18 semester units.

That's not a misprint. Seven dollars and fifty cents is all I paid for that virtually limitless buffet of classes, all of which counted toward my degree, which I completed at a state university. Then I went on to get my MA at State and my PhD on a partial scholarship for year one, and then on a fully paid assistantship for years two and three.

My MBA and JD were earned at expensive private schools. By the time I attended, I made enough income to pay for these out of pocket as I went.

To pay my living expenses, I took out federally insured student loans, which I paid back with ease after they became due. But they were deferred for years while I earned the MA and PhD.

This is worth a comment. Remember my economics professors at community college, who looked at us straight in the eye and made this suggestion:

Borrow heavily when you're young, because you'll be paying back in cheaper dollars!

What did he mean? For one thing, we can (almost) always count on a certain amount of inflation to make our currency worth less and less. When I did repay my loans, I was paying 7% interest on top of the principal I borrowed.

But the cumulative amount of inflation between the years I borrowed and when I repaid vastly exceeded 7%. Ultimately, I paid back in 25% cheaper dollars.

Plus my degrees became worth more and more as time passed because there was inflation in wages during that time as well.

As I write these words, there are proposals to increase the nation's deficit by trillions of dollars. This means inflation is around the corner, and the amount of it could be HUGE.

Instead of seeing a fairly normal 1–3% rise in annual prices, we could be looking at 10, 15, or even 20% price hikes.

If you are borrowing at fixed rates and paying simple interest, as you would with some student loans, then it could make sense to take my professor's advice, even if you don't consider yourself to be young anymore.

Borrowing heavily in the next few years could make perfect sense, especially if you are taking on good debt. You'll be paying it back in far cheaper dollars.

In such a context of rising prices, and what could be rapidly rising asset values such as real estate, it would be foolish to stay on the sidelines and not to borrow.

In such scenarios, the siren song that implores you to "live debt-free!" will take your little boat and crash it on the rocks.

Look at it this way. If you have zero debt, but almost the same paltry amount in income, what good is that?

Conversely, if you owe $100 million on real-estate assets that are providing you with a million dollars in net rents over and above your costs, you should sleep like a baby at night.

Inflation isn't kind to everyone. It hurts pensioners and professors and postal workers and others on fixed incomes who have no power to keep up with prices that are rising around them like floodwaters.

I'm saying we should read the tea leaves. They're telling us something important, just as my professor did to those of us lucky enough to be sitting in his class on the day he told us to borrow heavily.

To cap this discussion, it's true that I've said there is good debt and bad debt. But there are scenarios in which *all* debt is good or *all* debt is bad.

This should go without saying, but you shouldn't borrow from people that will break your legs or worse if you miss your payments. I'm speaking of loan sharks and the criminal element.

Typically, because they're operating outside the law, they don't have access to the court system, so they are barred from suing you to compel repayment. This means they'll use other means—unpleasant means. You can bone up on these by watching a few Martin Scorsese movies, like *Goodfellas*.

You don't want to stiff *THEM!*

Let's stick to legal debts, though. Generally speaking, at the earliest inkling that you'll never be able to repay your conventional debts, you face a decision:

Should I pay whatever I can, sacrificing most pleasures and indulgences, just to make minimum payments or even less? In other words, should I valiantly go down with the ship?

I'm going to repeat a story that I refer to in another section. You might be skipping around and may have missed it. If you caught it the first time, let this be a reinforcement of the learning point:

There is a woman that reportedly starved her children so she could make her minimum payments on her charge cards instead of having them canceled.

That's insane. It's also criminal child endangerment, among other reprehensible things.

But the story means that some people are so completely hypnotized into defending their endangered credit that they will endanger those near and dear to themselves instead.

Wow! With the retelling, I get short of breath.

Don't be a fool. Bad debt is any debt that you have no viable chance of repaying in a reasonable amount of time.

So if you read the fine print on your credit-card statements informing you how long it will take to pay them off, you might see 25 or 30 years. By that time, you will have repaid the principal amount you borrowed many, many times over.

Is there any way we can characterize a debt that lingers for two or three decades and that isn't a mortgage, as being "good?"

Especially if you incurred those charges by eating out at so-so, pricey, and trendy restaurants, treating your friends to food and drink, and paying for the privilege long after they gave birth to and raised kids and put them through college by NOT paying those restaurant tabs?

That's crazy too.

So when you get that faint but ever-stronger signal in your brain that you'll never, ever pay off those debts, they have already turned bad.

It's time to dump them and to stop trying to be a hero to the wrong people.

Look at the situation as you would a bowl of cherries. At first the bowl is filled with juicy, life-sustaining treats. Then you eat one after the next, and all that is left are the pits.

No matter how much or how often you try to buff and polish those pits, they'll never turn into cherries again.

Your bad debts may have been like those cherries, but now you're stuck with pits.

The sooner you see them for what they are and realize that your enjoyment of them is all in the past, the better off you will be.

Empty the bowl!

Search for new cherries.

Chapter 2

Tapping Your Negotiating Power

You have far more power than you know.

I'm speaking of negotiation power. This is the ability to make and remake deals of all kinds.

Most deals start with us. As I point out in my Best Practices in Negotiation classes at Berkeley and UCLA, the most important deals begin between our ears, in our minds.

It is there that we set our aspiration levels—what we hope to achieve and believe we can achieve. Great opportunities begin in your own mind. But this is also where most people fall short, far short, of getting what they really want and need.

Let me offer a modest example to illustrate this point. You go to a yard sale and see a bicycle that looks inviting. You're ambivalent: having started and stopped lots of exercise programs, you're not sure if you'll really use it.

So whatever money you put into it could go down the drain.

Still, you're intrigued.

"How much is this?" you inquire.

"That's $85, about half of what you'd pay for a new one," the owner replies.

Score a point for the owner, because she recited a price but also provided a frame of reference for interpreting it.

Half-price, you're thinking; not bad. But you'd love to do better, yet you don't want to be insulting.

So instead of haggling, going back and forth with offers and counteroffers, you say thank you, and you walk away.

In this scenario, you defeated yourself. Here are just a few things you should know.

The price someone wants to get for the bike, what she will accept for it, and what the highest bidder at the yard sale will pay, are three different things. And they aren't written in stone.

Indeed, the entire "value" of the bike is arbitrary and very fuzzy. We can say with a degree of certainty that it isn't worth what it sold for originally. Like a car, it has depreciated in value, if only because of wear and tear to the tires, to the seat, and to the frame and gears.

We can also say the bike is worth more than a few dollars if it is in working condition.

But you want to get something off the price; you want to get a deal of some kind, at least to assuage your concern that you won't get a lot of use from the item once you own it. Plus, if you can get a discount, it will make you feel savvy and clever. Above all, discounts help us to avoid getting ripped off completely.

But where do you start? How do you begin your counteroffering sequence?

There is a general rule that applies when setting a price: If you're buying, aim low. Underoffer if you can. If you're selling, ask for more than you'll be willing to accept.

So aim low or aim high, depending on your role as a buyer or seller. This is a best practice, and one of the most important.

In the bike situation, this does not mean replying to the recital of the $85 price with the request, "Would you take $75 for it?"

There's nothing wrong with the wording per se. But your price is way to high.

I'd ask a few questions about it, sit on it, ride it on the sidewalk. Then begin your spiel.

"Here's my situation. I'm really tight on money right now because I've had to change apartments. So I'm pretty much tapped out. My major concern is whether I'm really going to use it or end up giving it away or throwing it away." Long and thoughtful pause . . . "I don't mind investing $10 or $15 in it," you say.

Wow, you might be thinking. I'm really low-balling here, suggesting a really deep discount, considering where she started her pricing. That's a fraction of the $85 she started with, just over a sixth of the asking price.

Not to worry, because you need to leave room to come up in your offer if you really want the bike. In your mind you should be setting an upper limit you'll pay, and a lower price that you'll start with. Let's say you believe it is worth $50, tops, or at least that's the amount you're willing to fork over.

How are you going to mutually agree to $50? I can tell you how, in all probability, that *won't* happen. It *won't* happen by blurting out, "I can pay $50, tops."

I know, that's your bottom line and you're in a rush and you dislike haggling. But if you start at your bottom-line offer, you leave yourself no room to come up to counteroffer her first counteroffer. You will have painted yourself into a corner.

Let's take a closer look at the arithmetic. She asked $85. For her to match your walk-away price of $50, she'll need to give you a $35 discount. You won't achieve that much of a drop all at once.

If you start at $15, you can come up by $35 and hit your $50 target. So starting this low, you can actually arrive at an equal compromise price based on her first price. She'll come down $35 and you'll go up $35.

"No, I can't do that, sorry," the seller says. "I can give you twenty bucks off, though, which makes the price only $65. Will that help?"

Here is where another concept comes into play: how to split the difference. With this angle, you can do even better than getting the bike for $50.

"I'd love to give you that, but I really can't." (After some time . . .) "I'll tell you what. I'm willing to compromise with you. You're at $65, and I'm at $15. That's a $50 difference. If you come down $25 I'll come up $25, which will make the price $40. That's really a stretch for me, but that's fair, isn't it?"

Reread this portion, please. If you weren't paying really close attention, you probably overlooked some fun features.

First, I start with "I'd love to give you that, but I really can't." What's that about?

I'm trying to send a pleasant relationship signal and appear like a nice guy. It's good news, then bad news. By saying something congenial, I take the sting out of the not-so-good news to follow.

"I'm willing to compromise with you." This is a plus, because most of us have been taught that compromising is good: we give a little and get a little.

Pay special attention to how I discuss the numbers. I say, "You're at $65 and I'm at $15. That's a $50 difference." Was she really at $65, or was the number $85?

I'm saying she's at $65 because she came down to that number, so I get a much better compromise result using it instead of $85. I didn't come up from $15, so that's still my number.

If we split the difference between $85 and $15, that would amount to $70, or $35 each. Coming up by $35 would put me at my walk-away price of $50.

So if she counters with, "Wait a second. Let's split the difference between $85 and $15!" I can do that and still get the bike at an affordable price.

My goal in this extended example is to illustrate a few basic and critical concepts. As I said, aim high or low, depending on if you are buying or selling.

Also, craft your compromises so they tilt in your favor. Don't offer to compromise immediately. Get them to lower their price, and use that reduced number when you compromise.

Another takeaway is always remaining as pleasant as you can be. Saying "sorry" and "I wish I could" are softeners that make people more pliable and less resistant.

And of course this good stuff works on collectors and IRS folks, because, as quiet as this is kept, they are people too. Negotiating for other folks and for myself, I have found IRS personnel very decent to work with—competent and very polite.

In part this is because I avoid making them feel defensive by attacking them.

There are some messages you should avoid that promote hard feelings and vindictive responses. There are six in particular. First identified by researcher Jack Gibb, they are predictably explosive.

They are *evaluation*, *control*, *strategy*, *neutrality*, *superiority*, and *certainty*. Let's look briefly at each.

The epitome of *evaluation* would be name-calling, as in: "You idiot!" or "How dumb can you get?" Simply writing these down makes me laugh, because they're so outrageous. But people say mean things like this all the time, or they imply them.

I was shopping for a car. On a test drive with a salesperson, who was a son of the dealership owner, I made some kind of disparaging remark about the car.

"Why, this car is smarter than most people!" he snickered. Clearly, on that occasion he was not going to successfully supply me with a new vehicle!

Evaluation doesn't always have to include name calling. Just saying, "You shouldn't have done that" can do the trick, because people hear it as, "You shouldn't have done that, you nincompoop!"

Control is the next type of defensive message. This is conveyed when someone says, "There are rules you'll need to follow." Instantly we might think, "Not me, pal, you can't make me do anything."

This is an important thing to note when defensiveness enters the conversation. If they push our buttons, our reflex is to push theirs back. Defensive barbs elicit defensive reactions.

Remember when you were a kid and someone called you a goof or a bozo? Correct, that's *evaluation*. See, you're learning. How did you respond?

You probably whined back, "No, YOU'RE the bozo!" Between grown-ups, I can tell you that nothing about this knee-jerk response has changed.

If anything, when shoved (rhetorically speaking), we shove back harder.

I've got to tell you a story, because this just happened.

I was scanning my book and audio titles online, because I'm in the process of developing an author's page (www.drgarygoodman.com). Unexpectedly, I saw that someone bashed one of my books by giving it a "1" score, the lowest possible.

As I was reading his "review," it quickly became apparent that his ill will had zero to do with what he found in its 170 pages. He ranted about how one of my classes that he had signed up for, for which he had purchased a book, was canceled.

I had nothing to do with that, or with the fact that sometimes even the best sessions can underenroll, forcing universities to nix them.

I only had two scores online for that book, a 4 and his 1. So the average of the two make the product seem less than thoroughly appealing. Worse, if you Googled my name, that book and its depressed rating was the first search result you'd see.

Thus, without further scrutiny, it would seem I am a below-average author.

Maybe I don't have to tell you, my professional ego bristled. I've often noticed how people give undue importance to single scores. For years, bodybuilders were informed they were obese according to the BMI, the Body Mass Index. This is a single score that takes your height and weight and says whether your body mass is within or outside of healthy limits.

But it doesn't account for muscle. Muscle weighs more than fat. So your BMI could be bloated, but you could look as good as Mr. Universe, which is what Arnold Schwarzenegger was in the days when he reached what most described as physical perfection.

When we speak of debt, naturally the FICO score is mentioned. This is a single rating that says to lenders whether you are or are not creditworthy. Clearly, it doesn't accurately predict how you will do in paying back your loans, because it cannot see into the future.

It doesn't know whether you will be laid off from your job and be replaced by a robot. Likewise, it has no clue that you're due for a big raise, making your debts easier to service with regular payments.

The IQ score is notoriously flawed when it comes to measuring intelligence.

GPAs, grade point averages, can be wildly inaccurate. My undergraduate grades were lower than I would have liked because I was working full-time and going to school full-time. They didn't prevent me from doing a master's and then a PhD.

I applied to law school after having earned my doctorate. They didn't care what my grad-school grades were, which were practically all A's. They focused on undergrad performance. I had to argue that I had shown even more academic promise by mastering higher levels of intellectual challenge.

Getting them to overcome their one-score bias toward the undergraduate GPA wasn't easy!

At present, the Chinese government is devising a single score to assign to their citizens. This will supposedly assess their loyalty to the state. With a bad score, they'll be subject to being stopped in the streets and interrogated, or worse.

Clearly, single scores are flawed, and we overreact to them.

So when I was spied my book's online score, I was certainly defensive, feeling that the book and my course were going to pay a dear price for this unfair sliming.

But the stars were shining down on me. The guy left a clue, signing the review with what had to be his own name, a distinctive one at that.

As fast as you can say, "I'm going to talk to him!" I Googled and found several entries for that name. A few clicks, and I had some phone numbers. I called, left a message, and the assistant volunteered this critic's cell number.

Perfect. I called him.

He said it was actually his son, who has the same name, that signed up for the class; he must have been disappointed that it was canceled. The son probably took off a day of work and was disappointed the class didn't run as planned.

I said, "Please tell him there is another session opening up in April, and if he wants to arrange a refund of the book, that might be possible."

The papa said they were on a cruise! You've got to love that. I'm sure Junior never imagined he would be called on the carpet for the flaming he did online.

Having provided my email address to papa, I said that Junior should contact me directly to recant his bad review and have it taken down.

A day later, obviously after they had stewed about this, I got a note saying, "You're stalking me!" I wasn't, but that's beside the point.

I nearly wrote back a scathing missive of my own, talking about how they were defaming me, but I thought better of it and just decided to contact Amazon on my own to report abuse of their review platform.

In their defensive mood, a reply would only have added fuel to the flames of defensiveness contained in the accusation of stalking.

This sequence of being attacked and reflexively attacking back is universal. All of us succumb to it, some more than others.

When someone shoots a cannonball across your bow, you don't have to shoot back. In fact, the best way to counter an attack is by being supportive instead.

But I'm getting a little ahead of myself. Let's quickly finish up with the other four types of defensive messages first.

Strategy is the third of the six. If you asked an IRS agent, "Are you going to garnish my wages?" that would be a straightforward question. If stated with a neutral or friendly tone, it would not come across as defensive.

However, if the IRS agent replied, "Well, I can't tell you that," then you would have heard a strategic reply.

"You can't? I'm a taxpayer! What kind of heartless so-and-so are you?" is how you would like to respond. But as you know, what would then happen?

Exactly right. The IRS agent would blast you back, or recoil into a hateful silence while secretly vowing to write a nasty note in your file that would say to help you as little as possible.

Not because their character is flawed, but because they are human.

We're all put together the same way when it comes to these "You bite me and I'll bite you back" messages.

Superiority is the fifth defensive message. Pulling rank is one way of pushing this button.

Let's say you came to me for professional help, which I don't mind in the least. You're invited to contact me directly if you need additional help. (You can even review this book, *if you're nice*! No one likes mean criticism, right?)

OK, say that you came to me and asked, "I want to try this negotiation technique with the IRS; what do you think?"

If I were in a very grumpy mood and replied, "Well, in my decades of experience I'm never heard of that being used," that would sound definitely superior. And you'd be very human to find it offensive.

So much so that you might respond, "Look, that doesn't mean anything! You wish you had thought of this gambit yourself! You're not such a smart guy, after all, are you?"

OK. Let's say I'm in a good mood, or at least not grumpy. What then?

I would definitely *not* use number six on you, which is *certainty*. I'd choose to be *supportive* instead. I might say, "That sounds interesting. Give it a try!" That would be showing flexibility, which is the opposite of certainty.

I would not hear your idea and quip, "That'll never work!"

When we hear someone using certainty, suddenly our lives take on a new mission. We live to disprove that what the person is saying is an unassailable fact. We'll find the exception to his rule. If it takes forever and we have to quit our jobs and leave our loves, we'll show him up!

By succumbing to this crazy passion, we are actually expressing the same defensive nuttiness, vowing to prove to a CERTAINTY that he is WRONG in being CERTAIN!

In the real world, if there is doubt about your liability for a debt to a bank or to the IRS, you will want to point this out. For example, there is a provision in IRS policies that enables an "innocent spouse" to avoid liability for tax debts incurred by their spouse.

You'll want to stand up and say, "You're wrong. I don't owe that!" But there's a supportive way to do it and a defensive way.

The supportive way is to say, "I'm sorry, but I don't believe that is my tax debt. You see, my spouse was in charge of that, and he's to blame for any outstanding tax debt with regard to this matter."

Quick minireview: If another person uses certainty on you, resist the impulse to use it right back on him. Instead, select your words so they seem somewhat flexible—more tentative, rather than conclusive.

Here are the six supportive messages that are alternatives to defensive ones: *description*, *solution orientation*, *spontaneity*, *empathy*, *equality*, and *flexibility*.

In my seminars, I cap this section on defensiveness by offering a sentence that contains most of the supportive alternatives.

Let's say someone says, "You're wrong!"

You can keep your cool and reduce the negative atmosphere by replying:

"Gee, I'm sorry to hear you say that; let's see where we can go from here."

"Gee" is spontaneous. It doesn't sound strategic. "I'm sorry" is empathic. "To hear you say that" is descriptive and not evaluative. "Let's" implies equality: we're going to do this together, cooperatively. "See where we can go from here" is flexible. (I elaborate on this topic in another book, *Please Don't Shoot the Messenger!* It is published by Contemporary/McGraw-Hill.)

So far I have offered you these negotiation tips. Aim high or low depending on whether you are buying or selling. In debt resolution, make your offer as low as possible.

If you cannot afford anything, tell them, but nicely and not defensively.

Let me step back a giant step to help you understand why so many people fail at negotiating, especially on their own behalf.

The number-one reason is that they don't try. For one reason or another, they simply do not negotiate.

Let's say they're in a job interview, and they're offered $X to start. They won't try to improve that offer; they'll simply accept it.

This means they're leaving money on the table. When I was hired to be a tenure-track assistant professor at a leafy university, the pay was paltry, and I knew it would be. But I was still able to improve the initial offer by 10%, more or less, just by asking.

They probably knew I wouldn't walk away from their deal, but they wanted to appear to be reasonable and flexible, so they came up with a little extra to put into my pay envelope.

You might be thinking that banks and tax authorities are holding all the cards and you have zero clout. Nothing could be farther from the truth.

Especially if you're offering to pay something, anything, they should be thrilled right down to their toes. You could just hardball them and simply say, "Go fish!" and not pay a nickel.

So you need to change your mind-set if you believe it's "little me" or David versus Goliath. You are a powerful person who is simply tight on funding right now. And they'll need to understand that.

Bear in mind that most collectors have heard everything. If you can't pay, or you won't pay, this is nothing new. Join the parade of millions that are in the same circumstance.

If you're not in the mood to negotiate at a particular time—say you're in pain or you're distracted—then postpone or cancel any discussions you planned to have. You have to be in the right mood to take this on.

Let me give you an example or two. I had done a successful two-day presentation at Discover Card for its executives. Before I left their Arizona site, we spoke about expanding the program. That would have been quite profitable to me.

My consulting practice was solidly booked, so I was ambivalent about coming back. On the plane ride home, I hastily put together a proposal that, in retrospect, sounded defensive.

Naturally, taking offense, the company rejected my proposal.

A similar thing happened when I was speaking to JD Power & Associates about joining forces to offer some customer-satisfaction services. As I was leaving, a prickly lawyer who had attended my meeting with the CEO gruffly said, "We're going to need a nondisclosure/noncompete agreement."

This is pretty common, but I didn't like him or his demanding demeanor.

I barked back, *"So will I!"*

That defensive exchange didn't go over well, I can tell you.

I should have called a time-out, taking more time to consider the risks and rewards associated with both deals. In a word, I wasn't in the right mood to negotiate.

I suppose you could say I didn't have the patience to make a deal.

So get into the right mood.

Another common negotiation practice is to avoid offering first. Back to the bike at our yard sale we go. If you're interested in the bike, you shouldn't volunteer an offer right out of the blocks.

You might be willing to pay $50 tops, as we said. So if you start there and ask, "Will you take $50 for your bike?" you've probably made a mistake.

What if the seller thought she could only get $15 or $20 before you asked? Now all she has to do is nod her head and she has tripled her hoped-for price.

By offering first, shooting your mouth off, you have done yourself a great disservice, and now you'll have to pay far more than needed.

The same precept applies to debt and tax settlement. If you ask, "How little can we settle this for?" you'll at least hear a number you can work with. Even if the reply is "100 cents on the dollar!" you know where you stand.

Savvy negotiators have a walkaway price that they determine in advance. Say you owe $10K but you're willing to settle for a max of $3K. If they don't come down to that level or even ask less than this, you're out of there.

Leaving the table, as it is called, is quite often a smart move.

If you're at a car dealership and you've haggled back and forth and heard their "best price," then politely say, "Thank you, I'll consider it." As your feet carry you to the door, typically the seller will say, "Wait a minute, maybe we can do a little better for you. Have a seat."

Similarly, nothing says that you must accept an offer from a collector. You too can walk away, if only by ceasing your communications or terminating your conversation.

Feeling you'll be "the one that got away," they'll have an impulse to chase you with a better deal. Their ego is involved in the outcome, because they've already invested a lot of time in you.

By leaving the conversation, you have instilled a powerful doubt that says, "Maybe we'll never get this wrapped up." And most folks can't resist trying to tie up this loose end into a neat bow.

What you don't want to do is put yourself behind the eight ball by overpromising. In my dealings with IRS, I agreed to a payment plan of $500 per month, when $100 would have been more realistic and sustainable.

I paid it for a time, but inevitably I had to default on that repayment agreement. It was simply too rich for my poor budget at the time.

Later I got the remaining IRS debt discharged in bankruptcy proceedings, because it met the criteria. But the learning point is still not to overpromise and underdeliver.

Your money situation is a big part of the equation in determining the deals to make. If you overobligate, you'll be needlessly adding to your stress levels, which is never good. With stress can come ill health, and then your resulting incapacity makes you of less value to yourself and to everyone else.

So in cutting any deal, ask yourself, "Is this doable and livable?" How are you going to feel about this burden three, six, or even eighteen months down the line?

Having said this, I should note there are exceptions to the rule—times when you'll take on a greater burden than you can handle in order to achieve a more pressing goal.

If the IRS or the state's taxing authority has slapped a lien on your bank account or has started garnishing your wages, they have you up against a wall. You'll need to get those liens removed as fast as possible.

In that circumstance, agreeing to a repayment plan

at $500 a month could make sense simply to release you from those encumbrances on your income and assets.

And who knows? That $500 payment each month might just turn out to be something you can handle.

A guy owes money to a crusty pirate who is demanding repayment. The debtor says, "Give me thirty days, and I'll get you the money. In the meantime, I'll teach your parrot to sing."

Not being the fastest buccaneer in the fleet, the pirate says, "Why should I let you do that?"

"Because with a singing parrot, you can charge big money and earn far more than what I owe you!"

The pirate agrees, but a bystander who hears the exchange asks the debtor, "What good is making such an outrageous promise?"

"Look at it this way. I've bought thirty days. The pirate might die, and I'll be free of the debt. I might find the money to repay him. And if I don't, this parrot just might learn how to sing!"

Some negotiations work like this. You make a promise that you suspect or know you won't be able to fulfill. But it serves a greater purpose.

We should take stock here and get our bearings. The subtitle of this magnum opus is *Your Guide to Paying Zero Dollars to the IRS* and so on.

As I was developing this theme, I was tempted to use the words, "How to Be a Perfect Flake."

Because from one point of view, stiffing people on what you owe can be seen as a flaky thing to do. I don't believe that, but some do.

This reminds me of a scene from a very good movie with Paul Newman, Tom Cruise, and Mary Elizabeth Mastrantanio: *The Color of Money*.

Newman is a veteran pool hustler and Cruise is his young protégé. They walk into a billiards hall, and Newman quizzes the kid: "Do you smell that?"

"What, smoke?" Cruise replies.

"No, money," his streetwise girlfriend, Mastrantanio, rightly chimes in.

Newman turns to Cruise at one point and says, "You're a perfect flake!" to which his trainee is about to take offense.

Before he can, Newman explains, "But that's a gift!"

If you want to succeed in billiards, and in negotiations, it is also a gift to be, or seem, somewhat flaky. When you are, people feel smarter than you, and they're apt to make big mistakes that can redound to your benefit.

When you have set a goal to pay zero dollars, you know something your creditors don't. You can be certain about it, making it your chief goal, while they foster the hope that if they bug you enough or wait you out, you'll break down and pay everything or at least something.

Because you know that it's possible to stiff them, and because you're committed to reaching that end, you can relax.

Nobody can force you to pay if you haven't any money with which to pay or any assets they can seize and convert into cash. That saying "You can't squeeze blood from a stone" applies.

They'll cut you a huge amount of slack, especially if they think you sincerely wish to pay but cannot, at least right now, but you will someday.

It's a gift if you are officially unemployed. "Gee, I'm not working right now. I'm broke. I'm going to have to ask you to wait."

Who hasn't been unemployed? They've got to empathize with that.

And most will ask you, "Well, when do you think you'll be back to work?"

Between us, the return of Halley's comet is a more definite event than when you'll get your next job offer, right? How the heck can you answer that dumb question?

"Well, I'm really trying, but I don't know. I hope right away."

"Why don't I put down 'within thirty days,' and we'll check back with you, okay?"

The first goal of a collector, as I have mentioned, is to get a payment right now. The next best thing is a "PP" or a promise to pay on a definite date, say when your next paycheck is due.

But they'll settle for something made up, like that thirty-day suggestion, if they have to. As we saw in my dialogue here, they'll even make up something for you out of thin air to put into their tracking and callback system. They need to show that they tried, not that they succeeded. So give them something to justify keeping their jobs!

It's also a gift if you're a senior citizen living on Social Security. Typically, nongovernment entities cannot garnish your Social Security payments. The IRS can, but only up to a limit of 15%.

You can tell a collector, "I'm strapped, living on a tiny Social Security check. Sorry I can't give you anything, but that's the truth."

They might plead: "Could you even send us a token payment of say $5? You can do that, can't you?"

There is a good reason to say no: the statute of limitations on contractual debt. In most states, this is a four-year time period during which debts are collectible.

Listen to this carefully. *With most written contracts, such as credit-card and medical debts, if you have not paid anything for four years, you may disaffirm the debt.* The debt is not collectible by operation of law, and you can refuse to pay. This statutory period can vary from state to state.

However, if collectors trick you into making a partial payment even after the four-year period has expired, this will revive your obligation to pay!

(In another section I mention that there is a tax statute of limitations on IRS debt, which is ten years. That's different.)

Collectors of all kinds will try to cajole you into hitting up your grown kids and other relatives to pay them. Your children and your sister Hazel have no duty whatsoever to retire your debts, so resist caving into this ploy.

Of course, there are lots of folks that may have access to money, but it doesn't appear they do. They put their assets into the names of their children, or set up trusts where they or their relatives are the beneficiaries, and they are not the official owners.

Especially if you're filing for bankruptcy, if you have made these moves within six months of filing, you could get into trouble. The trustee might declare such transfers of assets to be fraudulent. That would make them available for liquidation by the court and subject you to potential criminal penalties.

So you have to be very careful if you're contemplating the hiding of assets, especially when considering filing for bankruptcy. I advise speaking to an attorney specializing in this field who has special knowledge of trusts and wills.

There are other devices for appearing to be broke. People commonly work in the underground economy. One way is to barter your skills for goods and services.

There are bartering clubs and associations you can join that bring people together for the purpose of exchanging value.

As I write this, Bitcoin and other nongovernmental currencies are gaining a lot of interest, mostly as speculative earnings vehicles. Like money, these money equivalents are ways to exchange all sorts of goods and services across international boundaries.

Because of their block-chain technology, transactions are tracked, but ownership is anonymous, making them very desirable to those that want to buy and sell while going unnoticed by governments.

Is Bitcoin the same as money, as far as governments are concerned? Your IRS debt is denominated in U.S. dollars, and this agency expects to get paid in this format. As of this moment, I doubt if they have acknowledged Bitcoin as a rival currency or if they're set up to accept it, even if you wanted to retire your debt to them this way.

Once you cash out your Bitcoin shares, converting them to dollars, they might technically be called income, but this raises a question that is both philosophical and highly practical:

If a tree falls in the forest far away and nobody hears it, does it still make a noise?

If your transactions, your labor, the products you're transferring, and the virtual money you're receiving for them, fly completely under the radar, are they still "real" and subject to seizure as far as your creditors are concerned?

Speaking of currencies, what if you're paid in euros or Swiss francs? Assuming these funds go directly from offshore companies into offshore banks, and your labor is invisible, can these funds be reached by domestic creditors?

The IRS might have the means to track them down. But will Citibank—or the collections company it has sold your credit-card debt to—be able to scout out your hidden funds?

I sincerely doubt it, especially if you owe them thousands and not millions.

The key here is that you cannot live so opulently that it will raise red flags that anyone can see. If your stated income is zero, or is very small—unemployment or Social Security income, for example—you aren't under the radar anymore if suddenly you become a big spender.

Why am I discussing these machinations with you in a unit on negotiation? It's simple.

Negotiations start in your mind, with your aspiration level. If you aspire to paying zero dollars back to various entities, you're also bargaining for a bit of a furtive life, where concealment comes with the package.

"How far am I willing to go to pay ABSOLUTELY NOTHING?" is a question you'll want to ask yourself over a nice glass of wine or hot cider in front of the fireplace.

I just finished reading a fascinating article that turns conventional economic theory on its head. It says we need to adopt a quantum theory of economic events, one that allows for and even predicts chaotic outcomes.

Traditional econ hasn't sufficiently addressed the gross distortions that regularly occur, particularly great recessions and depressions. Economies go hopelessly through boom-and-bust cycles, moving at heartbreaking speed from affluence to austerity. So how can you as an individual hold yourself to a higher standard of predictability and reliability than the economy at large?

In 2008–09, the biggest banks got into so much trouble that they were failing. Many went bust. How can they hold us to higher standards of economic performance?

They're money experts, and they failed. We're amateurs, and they expect us to succeed when and where they cannot?

That is the ultimate "Do as I say, and not as I do" hypocrisy.

You're reading this book or listening to it because you're probably in a situation where you really *need* to STIFF THEM.

Negotiate between your ears right now. Tell yourself, "I have the right to use all available means of avoiding and canceling these debts, and the sooner I do, the faster I will prosper."

You need to focus on the present. This is where wealth is, prosperity, a comfortable life, if these conditions are what you are hoping for. When you're burdened by debts, you're mired in the past.

Worse, they're robbing you of your future by distracting you from creating it.

Putting this into baseball terms, how can you be expected to steal second base when your foot is bolted to first? It's impossible to bemoan what has happened, to cry over spilt milk while setting the table for today's feast. My dad had a simple prescription:

"Gary, if something is bothering you, holding you back, cut it out of your mind."

Then, with a sweeping martial-arts type of gesture, he pantomimed what that looks like.

There is a scene in *The Bourne Identity* where Matt Damon's character is riding in a car with the woman who will become his partner. He complains, "I can't remember anything that happened before three weeks ago."

She quips, "Lucky you!"

Which, of course, is a wise, Zen kind of insight. More often than not, we let the past dictate our expectations for today. In negotiations I see this all the time.

We're used to getting a certain price for our services. Suddenly the market changes, there's a recession, and we're facing price resistance. Instead of yielding to the new reality, accepting what is being offered, and earning *some* income, we stew about how much better the old days were. We sacrifice the chance to sell that perishable commodity, our time, for some financial gain, and settle for no gain.

There is a maxim to help you to avoid this trap of the past, coined by author and guru Baba Ram Dass: "Be here how." Also the title of his book, it is a reminder that the "pleasantness of presentness" is a highly desirable and effective state of mind.

I mentioned that we negotiate with ourselves by setting our goals, our aspiration levels, what we're striving to achieve. Being here now helps you to detach yourself from the limitations of the past. Just because something has been a certain way doesn't not mean it must always be that way.

Just because you paid your bills on time—which I had done for decades before my meltdown—doesn't matter. That guy no longer exists, so he should not be setting the financial agenda.

If I had adjusted my attitude sooner, making it conform to what soldiers call "facts on the ground" instead of to memories in my head, I would have been far better off. I would have saved time and avoided personal anguish and regret. This different posture would have empowered me to do what I inevitably did—far sooner and more smoothly.

There are far more negotiation tips we could cover, which is what I do in my book, *Dr. Gary S. Goodman's 77 Best Practices in Negotiation*.

For now, let's review and summarize.

Your creditors, banks, doctors, hospitals, and credit sources of all kinds *will negotiate with you*. In some cases, all you have to do is wait in silence until you have missed four to six payment cycles in a row.

Some will spontaneously cut the debts in half if you pay them right away. You can counteroffer, and say you accept their plan, but you'll need to make payments. Then stretch out the payments, without paying more interest for as long as you can, to make them as low as possible.

We've said, don't overburden yourself with a commitment to pay too much. I cited the $500-per-month payment I made to IRS, which was too much. Again, the exception is when they have slapped a lien on your property or garnished your paycheck and you need to get these liens removed. Then it might be worth stretching to make a bigger payment—temporarily.

Of course, you may be in a situation where you can afford nothing. Don't allow the conversation with creditors to degenerate into a defensive exchange. You now know the six messages that trigger defensiveness: evaluation, control, strategy, neutrality, superiority, and certainty.

And you also know the six supportive alternatives that reduce and prevent defensiveness: description, solution orientation, spontaneity, empathy, equality, and flexibility. Here is phrase that embodies them all:

Gee, I'm sorry to hear you say that. Let's see where we can go from here.

You've learned to aim high or low in negotiating, depending on whether you are selling or buying. In reducing your debt obligations, typically this will involve offering far less than you otherwise think you should.

You also know that is it generally regarded as a mistake to offer first; it's better to let them do it. This way, you can benefit from their underpricing mistakes while not overpaying.

We've discussed the value of walking away from a conversation and from their "best offers." Like car sellers, many creditors will chase you with a better deal.

Above all, although you may feel you are in an inferior bargaining position, you actually have an ace in the hole: *they cannot get what you do not have.*

If your assets or income are nonexistent, or if, through trusts and lawful transfers or other devices, they are not reachable, then you know something they don't.

At the end of the game, they may end up with zero cents on the dollar as repayment.

You can stiff them, partially or completely, with relative impunity, while rebuilding your credit standing in fairly short order.

Knowing this should confer upon you a peaceful frame of mind. No matter how much you owe and to whom, remember the expression, "This too shall pass."

And you'll be on your way to a fresh start!

Chapter 3

Bankruptcy Is Good for You and Great for Your Credit

The framers of the United States Constitution crafted a wonderful and practical document. They were smart and forward-looking individuals, intent on building an enduring republic.

So they established bankruptcy front and center in the Constitution, in article 1, section 8. It appears where the essential powers of Congress are enumerated.

It's not a lengthy section, so I have pasted it in below. Note the other important and essential powers that are granted side by side with bankruptcy:

> *The Congress shall have Power*
>
> *To lay and collect Taxes, Duties, Imposts and Excises, to pay the Debts and provide for the common Defence and general Welfare of the United States; but all Duties, Imposts and Excises shall be uniform throughout the United States;*
>
> *To borrow Money on the credit of the United States;*
>
> *To regulate Commerce with foreign Nations, and among the several states, and with the Indian Tribes;*

> *To establish an uniform Rule of Naturalization, and uniform Laws on the subject of Bankruptcies throughout the United States.*
>
> *To coin Money, regulate the Value thereof, and of foreign Coin, and fix the Standard of Weights and Measures...*

Note that the framers of the republic didn't insert a lot of fluff into that document (unlike some contemporary authors I know). Everything is there for a reason. So why does the Constitution explicitly provide for the process of bankruptcy?

It is mentioned even before Congress's power to coin money, that's how significant it is.

It's there because it serves a crucial purpose.

Bankruptcy is an official cleansing of debt. It aims at providing debtors a fresh start, a chance to wipe the slate clean. It also gives them a way to cease any hounding or pestering from creditors.

Let's describe what happens when you are weighed down by debts. You are being called on to pay out more than you are taking in. If you have no savings or properties you can convert to cash, this is an impossible task—to pay more than you earn.

Technically, you are *insolvent*, which means you are already bankrupt in all but the name. What are you likely to do if you are forced to pay what you don't have and cannot reasonably get?

You'll get frustrated, to say the least. You'll be angry and distracted, and you won't be able to focus on earning money. That's not good for you or for your loved ones, and it's definitely not going to help your creditors to see a payday from you.

You may also get desperate, and desperate people do desperate things. They resort to taking shortcuts to get money. These can include criminal acts, violence, theft, and other things that injure other people and destroy property.

Society doesn't want that.

Plus, if you are penniless, you can't spend what you don't have. This means you are unable to play a full and proper role as a consumer in a modern capitalist economy.

Your lack of spending contributes to a lack of taxes, a lack of jobs, a lack of profits, and a lack of wealth.

Society needs people who can buy. It is in the interest of society to rehabilitate your ability to do this, so that you can spend, not only on the essentials, but on some luxurious, ridiculous, highly taxed goodies as well.

This means that society wants and needs a way to give you more credit, the very thing that probably put you into financial trouble to begin with!

The economy is like a hockey game. Two sides face off—in this case, buyers and sellers. The key is to be an active participant, to be on the ice. It is impossible to carry on if too many people are sitting in the penalty box.

Bankruptcy actually shortens the amount of time you're out of the economic game. Most people that get their debts discharged through Chapter 7 bankruptcy are flooded with new credit-card offers within six months; some see them as soon as sixty days. Lenders don't offer gigantic credit lines right away, and the interest rates are high, but the offers are there and easy to accept if you meet the minimum criteria.

But what if you don't go through bankruptcy? What then? Here's the irony.

If you are late in your payments or you have defaulted entirely, you can't get more credit. You may find your car-insurance rates going up, and leasing an apartment or buying a house could become very difficult, because your FICO credit score is so low.

Even getting a job is imperiled.

As long as you are not paying or late in paying or underpaying, your credit will suffer. In effect, you are almost completely shut out of participating in the economic world. Try booking a hotel or a car rental without a credit card; it's hard.

The upshot of this is that *it is better to go bankrupt sooner than later*, because your ability to get and use credit will be restored that much faster.

Putting it in the clearest possible terms: *bankruptcy is great for your credit*, because it enables you to get some! Without the official cleansing of debt, you will be an untouchable to banks and to other institutions.

Once you have credit again and you're paying as agreed, your credit limits will be increased, and you'll be able to borrow at better and better interest rates.

But you have to be wondering: why is there bad press associated with going bankrupt? Why is it made to seem like asking for a case of leprosy?

Good questions!

Banks and others want to max out their profits. The way to do this is to get you to make high-interest minimum payments for as long as possible. Check out the disclosures at the bottom of your credit-card statements.

If you make the minimum payment only, you'll probably be paying for twenty-five to thirty years! That's what banks want. If it becomes perfectly acceptable and even desirable to put a stop to their practically endless cash flow, they'll lose tons of income.

That's why bankruptcy is purposely conflated with morality. Creditors want you to believe that you are a bad person if you don't pay them every penny. If they can get you to accept this premise, they'll have you hooked forever.

Let me adjust the lens a little so you'll see this from a different viewpoint. I've been speaking about consumers and consumer debts here. Let's turn for a moment to business borrowing and business debts.

Society generally wants and needs innovators, entrepreneurs, investors, and risk takers. Many in his day thought Columbus's voyage to the New World was doomed. But he raised money from those that believed otherwise. They knew if he brought back spices and exotic items from far away, they could charge huge sums and get rich.

To succeed like this, they had to risk losing their entire investments. No pain, no gain—you've heard that. The companion phrase is *no risk, no reward*.

OK, so let's say Columbus came back empty-handed on his first journey and his investors gained no return on their financing. Would it have served society's purpose for Captain Chris to be thrown in jail or to get a minimum-wage job at the McDonald's of his time?

Not only no, but heck no, it wouldn't! Captains captain ships. They don't squander their training and experience doing odd jobs.

Bankruptcy is a mechanism for captains of opportunity who have failed. It enables them to put their pasts behind them and to smoothly navigate to their next venture. We want them on the water and not in dry dock in the same way that hockey players should be skating and not riding pine in the penalty box.

Seen in this way, bankruptcy equals rehabilitation. It restores our capacity to fully participate in our economic times.

We want people to operate at their highest and best uses. High performance and significant contribution provide them with incomes, which they save and earn. These in turn provide other people and organizations with *their* incomes (including banks), and the wheels of the economy keep turning. Standards of living rise.

"Won't going bankrupt seem like I'm declaring myself to be a failure, that I'm hoisting the white flag of surrender?"

If you put it that way, it tells me that you have some emotional concerns that should be addressed.

Epictetus, the ancient Greek philosopher, said that it isn't events that disturb us, but our interpretation of those events.

In itself, going bankrupt is a very straightforward process, which I'll explain in a few minutes. You'll understand it right away and be able to do an initial evaluation about whether it is the best thing for you now or in the future.

So technically, it isn't daunting. What you need to do is to work on is getting comfortable with it. If you do it and you aren't right with it emotionally, you'll pay an additional price, which should be avoided.

Let's spend a few minutes with our feelings about the process, especially if you are feeling a sense of dread or foreboding. Ask yourself this key question: "If I don't go bankrupt, will this debt be resolved in the ordinary course of events?"

This is a math question, plain and simple: Do you have enough money to put a meaningful dent in your debt by making payments on it? Or are you in a minimum-payment purgatory with no hint of ever emerging?

In other words, are you throwing all the spare money you have at the problem without making any headway? If you are, then the decision to move forward is almost already made for you.

There are bankruptcy alternatives, such as credit-counseling programs, that can structure a repayment program for you. The best kinds are typically nonprofit organizations that charge minimal fees for organizing and supervising the process.

What they'll do is prepare a plan with you based on your income and debts. They'll see how much you owe and look at your disposable income after essential bills are paid.

They'll contact your creditors, having worked with many of them in the past. And they'll get those creditors to stop or reduce interest payments, thus accepting less than what you owe as a payback amount.

The sum total of all of those debt payments will then be crunched down to meet your disposable income. Let's say you can spare $200 per month. Then your creditors will need to accept their share of this overall payment amount.

And you'll pay that amount for an agreed-upon number of years, typically three to five. However, during the payback period, you agree not to apply for more credit. So your ability to take on debt is zeroed out.

What happens to your credit score during that three-to-five-year period? It is not going to recover instantly. There are a few reasons for this.

First, you are not paying back as you agreed to do on the initial credit terms that govern your debt. Anything less than full and timely payment dings your credit score.

Restructuring that debt through a credit-counseling program isn't going to give you an instant bounce in your FICO score. Over the course of years, if you pay as agreed on that modified debt-repayment plan, you'll see your score gradually rise.

Compared to bankruptcy, which cleanses your debt with a big, fast dunking, you're slowly doing a spot washing.

When you do a budget with credit counselors, they won't leave room for a lot of discretionary spending, I can tell you that. You'll be living a monkish existence, maybe not warming yourself by candlelight, but all the same, it won't be opulent.

And that frills-free situation will persist for years unless you win the lottery and pay off the remaining debts at some point. (Just don't disclose that you had the money for lottery tickets!)

I should point out that many of these nonprofit credit-counseling agencies are funded by banks and by other financial institutions. Why would they do that? And isn't it a conflict of interest for them to be on the banks' team if their avowed purpose is to help you to get out of debt?

It's a cozy relationship, to say the least, and some debtors simply don't trust agencies to be looking out for them at the same time they're looking out for creditors. Essentially, the credit counselors are seeking to get back to the banks as much of the banks' out-of-pocket costs as is possible, which means getting you to pay as much as you can possibly afford.

This fact is something *for-profit debt-settlement companies* exploit when they invite consumers to sign up for help. Here's how *they* work. They purchase lists of people with declining credit scores and a certain amount of debt, typically over a threshold amount such as $5000 or $10,000. They'll send them a teaser letter or email inviting them to get a loan "consolidation." This is borderline fraudulent.

A consolidation typically pays off your old debts and issues a single, new debt with new repayment terms. Such loans exist, but typically you need decent credit to qualify for them. If your credit profile has eroded, why would a new lender step in to pay your existing loans if it might lose everything with a potential bankruptcy filing?

Makes no sense.

So, taking the bait that your loans will be paid off, you respond to the invitation and are switched to a loan-modification program. In this program, private firms do more or less the same thing that nonprofit counseling agencies do.

After you sign up, they call your creditors and negotiate crunchdowns of your debts. They then charge you a percentage of what they save you on the reduced principal of your loans.

Example: Say you owe $10,000 to various credit cards. The private loan-modification firm persuades them to accept $6000. Pretty good so far, isn't it? But wait, there's more.

Typically, you will be charged 35% of your *savings*, which is 35% of $4000. That comes to $1400 in fees. So, instead of saving a full $4000, you'll actually save $2600 on that $10,000 in debt. You'll repay $7400, which is a reduction of 26% on your original credit-card obligation.

You'll be given a payment plan, and let's say it is $200 per month. You have to meet that obligation for a stated number of months. What happens to your credit while you're making payments?

Again, as with using a nonprofit agency, your credit score will very slowly recover.

Generally it is more advantageous to use a nonprofit than a for-profit firm, though the latter will try to convince you they are better negotiators, and are therefore able to deliver an enhanced result: lower payments and a shorter repayment term.

But the best way to proceed (outside of bankruptcy) is this: if you feel you must pay some amount back to creditors, *settle your debts by yourself*. Using the example above, if you're able to reduce the debt from $10,000 to $6000, then you'll save a full $4000, which is 40% off your original obligation.

Rest assured, you can probably do better in regard to reducing principal, interest, and repayment terms if you use a do-it-yourself solution.

In a Chapter 13 bankruptcy proceeding, unlike a Chapter 7, you are actually required to pay back a portion of your debts to qualifying creditors under the trustee's supervision. In a 13 filing, you must follow a repayment plan to the letter for your debts to be discharged, and typically up to five years of repayments will be available.

In simple terms, in a Chapter 13 filing, you'll submit proof of your income, expenses, and debts and also submit a repayment plan that either partially or completely repays your obligations.

I believe Chapter 7 is a better way to go, if you qualify. There are income limits and asset requirements that may compel you to use Chapter 13 instead. Determining which way to go and what exactly you qualify for is how bankruptcy attorneys earn their money, and justifiably so.

Speaking of attorneys, there are practical and even legal limits on what they can charge you in order to have their fees approved by the trustee. If they exceed the guidelines, their fees will come into question, and they'll need to argue persuasively to the trustee to get them approved.

Why have we explored filing bankruptcy in this early chapter, when so many people and pundits regard it as a last-ditch, "when all else fails, do this" proposition?

I've put it here because it may be the best course of action for you *right now*. What benefit is there in hesitating, in making valiant, superhuman, but already doomed gestures to vanquish your debts?

Every payment made could, if you are in dire straits, take an additional crumb off your plate or a pair of shoes from your children's feet. (As I mentioned, there are horror stories of parents who have starved their kids in order to make minimum payments on charge cards!)

As you may know, according to Elisabeth Kübler-Ross, an authority on dying, there are five stages people move through in handling grief and hard times. The first is *denial.*

We don't want to consciously acknowledge that we're in financial difficulty. I've heard numerous debtors say, like Pollyanna, "Oh, one day I'll just pay it all off!" when they have no realistic means of doing so.

This is also known as *whistling past the graveyard*. We distract ourselves from the urgency of our circumstances. We have the sinking feeling that we have to act, but we deceive ourselves into believing it's OK to put it off, or we fancifully choose to believe that our troubles will vanish by themselves.

"Why did I wait so long?" is what many actually come to ask after they have had their debts discharged through Chapter 7.

In some cases it is because on an unconscious level

they believe they deserve to suffer, that suffering is a way to demonstrate contrition. Therefore it is redeeming.

Back to that wonderful document we go, to the Constitution. It guarantees three things: life, liberty, and the pursuit of happiness. Let's highlight number three—that quest to be happy.

Unless you are wired differently from most people, happiness and suffering don't go together. When you're in debt and not paying your bills, you get to meet a lot of folks that are nasty to you.

They're bill collectors, and they'll incessantly remind you that you owe money to them or those they work for. This is annoying and rude and is an ongoing interruption of your pursuit of happiness.

There are three ways to get them to relent: (1) Pay in full, immediately. This is probably out of the question for you. (2) Make a payment arrangement with them, of the entire amount or of a reduced amount that you can negotiate. (3) You can stiff them—not pay them anything.

If you opt for stiffing them, you can do it by avoiding them or by jettisoning them through bankruptcy proceedings.

Let's discuss silence. They'll call you and write to you. They'll notify credit bureaus that you're late. Then, within about four to six months, that late status will become a "defaulted" status.

Defaulting makes your FICO score quickly and deeply plummet.

When this happens, much of the harm to your credit has already occurred. From the view of potential creditors, you are not worthy of receiving added credit. You will pretty much be on a cash basis with your bills, being unable to spend more than you take in from your income sources.

If you are used to spending freely using plastic, this cold-turkey situation is shocking. And it puts you in a precarious spot.

Those threadbare tires your car has been running on may blow out, requiring immediate replacement. How will you swing that expense without plastic? Or you'll take a job that requires overnight travel and the submission of credit-card receipts for reimbursement. How do you explain having no plastic, needing to be advanced all your expenses in cash or on the company's card?

It's embarrassing, to say the least, and it could be life-threatening if your car needs repairing or vital maintenance.

I'm trying to be anything but cavalier here. *Stiffing your creditors will have consequences.*

But note this: paying them as agreed will not necessarily get you more credit than you have. If your income is inadequate and your expenses are too many and you owe too much, you could be maxed out without the capacity to obtain more credit.

Happily, there are some solutions—imperfect, but helpful. If you don't make those minimum payments and you save some of those dollars, you can purchase prepaid debit cards, which can be used in much the same way as a conventional Visa card, and may even bear the Visa logo.

Carrying one of these with you with, say, $200 to $500 in stored money on it, you can brave the roads and book and pay for hotels. In this sense, you're not completely shut out from spending the way normal folks do, and the way you did before you went financially underwater.

We were speaking of going silent with regard to your creditors. I was saying they'll pester you, with emails, voice mails, live conversations if and when you answer the line, and with conventional snail mail.

If your debts are large enough, some creditors and collection agencies will eventually sue you in court to get a judgment that can be used to attach your assets and liquidate them, or to garnish your wages, compelling repayment that way.

If you have no assets and you're out of a job, there's nothing for them to latch on to. In this condition, you are what is known as *judgment-proof*. It means, "Go ahead and knock yourself out. Spend money suing me, but at the end of the day, you'll get nothing and you'll be out of pocket, having thrown good money after bad."

Informing creditors of your judgment-proof status may deter them. But many collection agencies are mills that grind through thousands of cases, and they may get a judgment nonetheless in the knowledge that if you win the lottery or one day acquire new assets, they can seize them.

Typically, judgments are obtained by sending you a legal notice that you are being sued. If you do not file what is called an Answer, they'll file for a Default or

Summary Judgment. That piece of paper will "perfect their financial interest" in the debt you owe, and it will enable them to sell your stuff, hack your wages, and be on the lookout for a financially richer you in the future.

But you can negotiate with them even on the courthouse steps, as the expression puts it. They may accept far less than you owe, and why?

They paid a pittance for your debt from the original company that you owed it to.

Probably they paid pennies on the dollar. So, if you say, "I'll pay you half," they'll lick their chops after shedding some crocodile tears and going back and forth. Then they'll gladly grab it.

Knowing they have so little at stake, you may get away with offering them 5–20% if they truly believe you're judgment-proof.

But your best lever in the game of negotiation is a viable, logical, and rational threat of going bankrupt.

If they think they run the risk of losing everything, they'll become much more pliable. Yet even this is not certain, because there is an antifraud provision in the bankruptcy law.

If you have given preference to one creditor over another by paying them money within six months of filing your bankruptcy petition, that money can be disgorged by the trustee and be distributed to other creditors. Or it could be distributed among the creditors in various proportions based on the priority given their liens on the bankruptcy "estate."

The net of this means that savvy creditors may not bend to your bankruptcy threat, because they know they'll have to give up what you pay them, unless you file later than six months after any transfer to them.

Still, the threat may be worth a try.

You may need to reach for the big gun anyway: filing bankruptcy as a creditor-management device.

As I mentioned, the bankruptcy court places an automatic stay on creditors when they receive official notice of the filing of your petition. This is a legal notification that says: stop all collections efforts immediately. The trustee manages the petitioner's estate, which includes all assets and debts. Each creditor's rights and interests will be settled in an orderly and fair manner.

If creditors ignore the stay and they contact you anyway, you can sue them for money damages.

The stay isn't indefinite. Typically it is in force for three to six months while your case works its way to resolution. If your case falls out of bankruptcy before a discharging or rescheduling of your debts, by your failure to comply with the court's requirements, or by withdrawal of your petition, or by another instrumentality, creditors can resume hounding you.

I need to make something clear. *Bankruptcy trustees are nobody's fools.* They're savvy and sophisticated, and you are not going to con them.

Even if you are a financial Houdini, do not try to hide assets from them. First, it is unlawful. Hiding assets is fraudulent, and you can be fined and imprisoned.

Even if you have some assets—and I'm assuming they don't amount to very much—you'll probably be able to legally keep them. Depending on their types and amounts, they will fall under certain court-recognized exemptions.

In some states there are catchall, wild-card exemptions available as alternatives to itemized exemptions for your car, clothing, furnishings, jewelry, and home equity. Wild cards enable you to keep a total of around $20,000 of personal assets and cash out of the bankruptcy estate. In California, this amount is currently about $24,060. (This is only part of the exemptions story, so you need to get expert help in determining what assets are exempt in your specific situation and locale.)

But in fact, instead of acting fraudulently, hiding, or erroneously minimizing the value of assets, people tend to do the opposite. They go out of their way to overvalue their holdings, which is foolish.

For instance, furniture costs a lot of money when we buy it off the showroom floor. A couch can easily cost $5000 or more, especially if it is upholstered in leather and it is a sleeper with a bed in it.

In our minds, that's a $5000 asset long after we've purchased it and used it. But the court does not see it that way. The court asks this question: "What would it bring in a liquidation sale?"

This means what could you reasonably charge in an everything-must-go fire sale?

If you parked that couch on the sidewalk, you'd probably be lucky if someone would take it off your hands for free! Worse, you might have to pay to have it taken to the local dump by a driver who charges by the trip, adds dumping fees, and so forth.

So what is it really worth in a bankruptcy setting? My guess is something entirely nominal, such as $5, maybe $10.

If you're laughing, I'm glad. This means you're seeing something ironic in this, and that's good. Most of the things we consider assets are practically worthless, and they may actually cost us money to relinquish them.

Driving from the beach yesterday, my eagle-eyed wife spotted a small sailboat in dry dock, with a sign attached that said, "FREE!"

"They're probably are tired of spending the monthly rental fees to keep it there," I said drolly.

Again, my point is don't hide or fail to declare your assets. At the same time, make sure to value them properly. Otherwise you do yourself a disservice.

Your car is another item that is probably worth far less than you think. Even if you have babied it over the years, most likely it would be classified as being in poor to fair physical condition. Prideful beings that we are, you may be thinking, "You're crazy, man. My ride is perfect."

Take it to some car dealers and ask them what they'll give you. That will be an eye-opener. I was going to trade in a car for a lease on a new one. I checked out the Kelley Blue Book and Edmunds, two reasonable sources for ballpark valuations. They told me that my car was worth about $11,500 at a dealership and about $14,500 to a private party.

The dealer I went to offered me $5000. "That's crazy!" I told him and stormed off the lot. I owed about $12,500 on it, so anything less than that was a nonstarter for me.

But it is a lesson in valuing cars. If you want a quick sale and you take it to a dealer, then that's what you will get, or even less. Their offer may be contingent on your buying or leasing a new car, and it will be thousands less if you don't.

Get these offers in writing, if you can, whatever they are. If not, you can still tell the trustee what you have been quoted, and he or she will sense whether it sounds right.

The learning point here is that gizmos and must-have items, like that snazzy couch, quickly end up being practically valueless. But you may have put them on cards that charge an exorbitant amount of interest. So, with compounded interest, the debts they incur get pricier and pricier. Think about that!

In a very real way, bankruptcy is a cleansing of illusions. You come to see that "stuff"—and I mean this in the very best George Carlin sense—is expensive clutter. We're tricked into thinking we need or want it by savvy marketing and high-pressure selling tactics, and by a culture that is constantly shouting, "Enough is never enough!"

So we get it, and the sooner the better! On credit, which means there is no pain right away. Gain without pain; now that's nice, isn't it?

Then the suffering starts. "Why did I ever buy this?" we remorsefully ask ourselves. Our candid friends and relatives inquire, "Who *sold* you THAT?"

If bankruptcy can lead you to a door with the sign on it that reads, "THRIFTY IS BETTER," then it will have been a very valuable process for you. Take clothing, for instance.

Wearing something out instead of throwing it out is a forgotten virtue your grandparents might have spoken of. I have white, long-sleeved shirts that we have probably washed a thousand times or more.

That's about ten years of washing, I suppose. Which means I have owned and used these shirts practically since the dinosaurs invented detergent. I'm proud of this, and before they get a second shot at living the good life as hand-me-downs or rags for finger painting, I bet I can squeeze out another hundred washings.

The manufacturer guaranteed only fifty. Why so few? To set my expectation level at a figure that would make me buy again sooner, earning that company more sales and quicker profits.

The austerity you are experiencing now, which is leading you to filing for bankruptcy, is a *gift*. It can reset not only your payment obligations but also adjust your consumption patterns for the better.

Charge cards should really be nicknamed *impulse cards*. They enable and encourage rash spending at the spur of the moment. When you file for bankruptcy, you will be relieved of most if not all of the cards still in your possession. You'll receive written notifications that they are canceled.

I've already noted the downside to not having a credit card for travel and emergencies. But not having that purchasing power keeps you from making dumb, impulsive buys over and over again. That discipline is more valuable than suffering to make minimum payments to keep those credit cards in your possession.

Let me caution you against something else before you file. Let's say you have $500 or even $2000 of remaining credit available on your cards.

Should you tap it, spend it, and then file right away?

No. That could be considered fraudulent.

Part of this depends on when these events occur. If you run up all of your cards on Tuesday and then file on Wednesday, this looks highly suspicious.

But if there is a gap of three to six months, and, especially if you're using your credit lines for groceries and essentials instead of for that airline ticket to Hawaii, you'll probably pass muster.

Seeing that your financial circumstances are eroding, and bankruptcy could be a move you are going to explore, should you charge another book or two on the subject from Amazon or your friendly bookstore? Why not?

Again, if your payments prefer one creditor over another or if your purchases are thought of as fraudulent, they will, minimally, not be discharged in bankruptcy. They will survive it, and you'll have to pay full value on them, plus potential fines and penalties.

Egregious frauds can also incur criminal culpability.

So let's review the highlights. I placed this chapter on bankruptcy early in this book, because it should not always be considered a last resort, as it is so frequently characterized.

Indeed, the sooner you pull the trigger, the better off you'll be, financially, emotionally, and even creditwise.

I noted that you should expect to see solicitations for new credit cards within six months of your bankruptcy discharge. Some have seen new offers as early as a few weeks afterwards.

Therefore the sooner you take the bath, the faster you'll emerge clean and ready to take on new debt. (I say this with a sardonic smile.)

How do you know the timing is right for you?

If you're upside down now, meaning that your obligations are greater than your income and disposable assets, that's a hint you should file for bankruptcy protection.

Also, if you've done the arithmetic, and you can see that (1) you can't repay your debts now, (2) making minimum payments is a huge stretch or involves substantial sacrifice, and (3) at the end of your efforts you will still be saddled with a debt load that isn't decreasing, then it sounds like bankruptcy is for you.

In a sense that is almost poetic, it's easy to imagine why bankruptcy is a natural fit for us, and why it ended up as a right guaranteed in the Constitution.

Our country has always been a land of second chances, and this unlocking of financial shackles is an embodiment of that promise.

It may be your time to break free.

Chapter 4

Getting the Tax Relief You Need

First, some good news: almost everyone qualifies for tax relief of some kind.

I say *almost*, because there are exceptions. If you have committed fraud on a grand scale, then the IRS isn't going to look fondly upon your request for help. Yet even in cases where you have done wrong, for instance claiming the Child Tax Credit when you have no children, in most cases the IRS will seek to be repaid for your false deduction, along with interest and penalties.

But they may not prosecute you criminally, which is a gift.

Another place where *almost* applies and you won't get any sympathy, is when you are labeled a *tax resister*. Tax resisters, as the term implies, are folks that believe the United States government has no authority to compel withholding and other tax payments.

The belief is informed by the idea that the income tax is unconstitutional. I'm not going to get into a debate about this, because the federal income tax has been with us for more than a century. And no amount of protesting is going to undo the need for the government to pay its bills. You might gripe about the high taxes we pay in the U.S., but with the recent reform legislation passed by Congress, the effective rate we pay is small, especially compared to European countries.

Whatever your private beliefs are, *don't gripe to any tax collector*! It's more than stupid, it's positively self-destructive. You're saying to them, "You have no right to do your job!"

How would you respond to that sort of attack? The answer is *defensively*, which we have already discussed.

If they label you a tax protester, they'll want to make an example of you, and if they can, they will prosecute you for tax evasion, which is a crime. Remember, the FBI did not nail the infamous gangster Al Capone for bootlegging or murder. They got him on tax evasion, and he died in prison.

Let me point out an important distinction. As a citizen, it is your right to lawfully minimize your taxes. This is called *tax avoidance.*

But it is illegal and outside of your rights to *evade* paying your taxes.

Tax avoidance is legal. Tax evasion is a crime.

Example: If you have a legitimate home-based business, you can deduct a portion of your rent or mortgage for the amount of space your business uses in your home. This is acceptable tax avoidance, utilizing all available and applicable deductions that pertain to your circumstances.

But if you have no business to speak of, and you are claiming a deduction that you are not entitled to, this is tax evasion, and it is punishable. *Don't commit tax evasion!*

There are far better, and perfectly lawful, ways to zero out your tax debts, which I am going to cover.

My CPA once gave me this advice: "Gary, earn as much money as you can and don't worry about whether you can deduct this or that. When the time comes, we'll protect your earnings." Meaning: report all income, but take advantage of all pertinent deductions.

For our purposes, I am adding something else. Vigorously explore ways to get your taxes lowered or forgiven completely if you have been saddled with a tax bill you can't handle.

There is as entry barrier to obtaining tax relief that I need to point out. Generally, to qualify for a reduction in the amount you owe, *you'll need to file all of your back taxes for the past ten years.*

How can you do this when you don't have receipts or W-2s? If you're utterly disorganized, it might seem impossible to document all of your income and expenses.

But this is an exaggerated concern. First of all, the IRS might have already computed some of the tax returns for you. This sounds like a gift, right? It is and it isn't.

The IRS uses the information about you that it has on hand when it does your taxes. This means it gathers the information submitted by your employers during a given year, including W-2s, to arrive at an income figure.

Then it applies the standard deduction for which you seem to qualify. That's it. If your income was so low that the standard deduction entitles you to pay no tax for that period, then you owe nothing.

But you will not get the benefit of itemizing deductions. They won't do a long-form tax return for you, giving you credit for a home office or gas mileage or other deductible expenses.

If you like, you can hire an accountant to redo those tax returns that the IRS did on your behalf. This makes perfect sense if you can prove that you had a lot of legitimate expenses, thus significantly diminishing your overall liability.

But you'll still be facing penalties for late filing and for interest that has accrued during the intervening period.

How can you learn what the IRS knows about you and your situation? You can request a *tax transcript*. Call the IRS and tell them what years you would like to see. They'll send you a printout of your tax status for those time periods. If you use a tax-resolution firm, an attorney, a CPA, or an enrolled agent to represent you, this will be the first step they'll take after speaking with you. They'll ask you to grant them a limited power of attorney, giving them authorization so they can proceed.

Alternatively, they may also have you be a party to a three-way phone call with the IRS in which you voice your consent, so that tax information can be shared during that conversation. This is to determine exactly what they say you owe. In effect, they're reading the tax transcript to you in real time.

Your representative will explicitly ask the agent, "Do you see any unfiled tax years?" And this will tell you right off the bat whether you'll need to do back-tax returns for given periods.

Some remedies are the low-hanging fruit of tax resolution. These are practically gimmes—yours for the mere asking. If you seek one of these, you may not be required to file all of your prior returns, at least not right away.

The easiest thing to request is a *payment plan*.

Let's say you owe $12,000 for accumulated back taxes. You've received a demand for payment by the IRS. They are threatening a bank lien or levy or wage garnishment. So they have gotten your attention!

If you phone them within the allotted time stated in the letter, you can tell them it is not possible to raise $12,000. "Can we arrange a payment plan?" is your first question.

In 99.9% of cases, those words will be music to the agent's ears. You've just stepped up, saying you want to retire this debt, and they do have the authority to bargain with you about the amount of your payments.

In this scenario, don't expect them to diminish the amount you owe. That involves a different remedy and documentation.

As we discussed in the chapter on negotiation, it is best to get them to make the first offer.

Tell them, "I'd like to make payments if I can, but unfortunately I can't afford much. How much would my monthly payment come to?"

They'll ask you a few questions about your income and expenses before shooting you a figure.

You should know that most payment plans are limited to 60 months: 5 years. So if they say you owe $12,000, what is that figure divided by 60? That's $200 a month—without interest. You know going in that $225 will probably be their bottom line, but they'll start with $500.

Should you just jump to $225 yourself? I don't advise it, especially if in truth you cannot afford it. Why paint yourself into a corner?

Reply, "Maybe I could do $100. Can we start with that and increase it after a year or so?"

They may give you a graduated payment, but they'll need a rationale to justify it. If you've been unemployed but hope to get a job within that time, this will fit the bill, no pun intended.

If your great-great-grandpa is about to meet his Maker, and you know for a fact that he has written you into his last will and testament, you can mention it. Any ray of sunshine over the not too distant horizon can justify a lower payment.

Now I've said this is a DIY—a do-it-yourself solution. It is, and you're capable of getting some kind of payment plan all by yourself. If you call a tax-resolution firm, they'll justify their fee by saying they're professional negotiators. They may even claim that they have former IRS agents on staff that will represent your cause and that they are definitely more skilled than you are. This could be true.

But remember, if the best they can do it to get you a 60-month repayment plan, what value are they adding by charging you, say, $1000–$2000 to set this up?

Here's what you should know. This bit of advice applies to hiring attorneys as well. They are trained issue-spotters. They went to law school and invested years analyzing cases where they needed to determine *every* issue and *every* remedy that applies to a given fact pattern.

They don't assume one size fits all. They aren't thinking, "We'll do a payment plan, because it's easy and quick." They're thinking, "What's the best resolution available to this person given his or her circumstances?" They're going to be more thorough and exhaust all possibilities, seeing opportunities and obstacles that are invisible to you. They could very well arrive at the conclusion that the best fix for you right now is a payment plan. The old joke applies. If you give a child a plastic hammer, then everything will look like a nail.

If you leave this book with the idea that a payment plan is low-hanging fruit that you need no help in plucking, then you're oversimplifying.

What paid representatives can also do is visualize a *sequential remedy* for you. Unless you've actually worked in tax resolution, this big-picture ability to conceptualize strategies will elude you.

Here's an example where really knowing what you're doing can save money, time, and hassles.

You owe $12,000, as we've imagined. But the great bulk of that liability stems from a tax period seven years ago. With a few exceptions, there is a ten-year statute of limitations on IRS collections. The IRS can attempt to collect your unpaid taxes for up to ten years from the date they were assessed. Once the ten years are up, the IRS can be compelled to stop its collection efforts.

If you can achieve currently not collectible status (CNC) for the next three years, you might not pay a penny on that liability.

Why pay anything when you can pay nothing?

Let's do some math. The tax firm said they'd represent you for $2000. To do a simple payment plan, that is excessive.

But compared to paying back $12,000 plus interest over 60 months, suddenly $2000 looks cheap. Doesn't it?

And yet it would be ideal to stiff the tax-resolution firm as well. Correct?

There are two ways to do that. (1) You can request CNC status directly with the IRS; and (2) you can request a payment plan from the tax resolution firm *for its fees.*

Let's start with (1). There's paperwork to fill out. You'll need to fill in an income and expenses form provided by IRS. You'll list everything: all sources of support. And then you'll show your expenses, along with applicable receipts and bank statements.

There aren't any surprises here. You'll see what you would expect: rent, utilities, auto, food, and so forth. Basically, if your income equals or is below your ALLOWED expenses, then you'll qualify for CNC status.

Note that I emphasized ALLOWED expenses. Based on your locality, the IRS has certain guidelines for allowable expenses. You might be paying $3500 for rent, but the IRS may only credit you with paying $3000.

There is a computer program that many accounting and tax-resolution companies use called IRSLogics. When you're on the phone with an intake representative, who might go by different titles, including "tax counselor," they will input the expense and income data as you speak.

With a click of a button, they can tell you what tax reduction you may qualify for. You may not have to pay anything at all. And if you do, they'll have a dollar amount that your data says you can pay—in the eyes of the IRS.

Their quotes aren't binding on the IRS. No tax firm can say, "You MUST give my client such-and-such relief." Likewise, no firm can predict exactly when or if your specific resolution will be approved.

Some things are faster than others. As I implied, setting up a payment plan might be a matter of making a phone call if you and the agent can come to agreement on a payment amount.

CNC status may take thirty days or more to get approved, because you need to submit income and expense itemization and receipts.

An offer in compromise, which is the big jackpot of tax negotiation, takes up to nine months to set up. I say it is the jackpot, because this is where you might end up paying pennies on the dollar on your tax debt, as radio ads sometimes promise.

Seldom is the settlement this good, but you may be one of the lucky people that has had a very bad run of financial luck. Let's say you made a lot of day trades of stock during the recent incredible bull market. Each short-term gain you realized triggered what is called a *taxable event*. Meaning that you owe money on your short-term gains, on your profits. That's not a surprise, but when the tax bill comes due, it could be a sizable sum.

After that, you plunked your money into a dumb investment that tanked. Now your wealth is gone. You have no significant income or assets you can tap. And the tax collector wants to be paid IMMEDIATELY. What do you do?

Well, you try to line up CNC status, because right now you have zero discretionary income to apply to the debt. This will buy you a year of relative peace. During this time, you should try to arrange an offer in compromise, because that can take nine months or more to approve.

By then you'll have *some* income—not much, but some. That will be what you can use.

Let's say you owe $100,000. In a standard repayment plan, this would mean that you're on the hook for $1666 a month for 5 years, plus interest. If you're showing only $170 a month in disposable income, this could reduce your debt by 90%.

Instead of having to repay $100,000, you'll be looking at something closer to $10,000.

These examples are offered not only to reveal some of the resolutions available to you, but to highlight the fact that they should be worked together so you'll get the greatest benefit.

Up to this point, we've discussed (1) payment plans; (2) currently not collectible (CNC) status; (3) offers in compromise; and (4) the statute of limitations on the collectability of tax debts.

There are other forms of relief available. One is called innocent spouse. The idea here is if a former spouse incurred a tax liability that the other spouse was unaware of and did not consent to, then the "innocent" spouse may be able to avoid liability for repaying that otherwise joint obligation.

There is also a kind of relief known as tax-penalty abatement. Let's say you failed to file your taxes during one of the previous ten tax years. The IRS discovered this lapse and has sent you a bill. That bill, as mentioned earlier, includes its estimate of what you owe, based on its actual knowledge of your income and/or the income it imputes to you.

Plus, the IRS tacks on interest charges from the time your taxes were due to the present. In addition, it socked you with a tax penalty, which is a charge to discourage folks from failing to file in the future.

As a general practice, the IRS will grant a one-time penalty abatement as a courtesy, providing it has not granted one to you in the past.

I should point out that you might want to actually file that missing tax return, providing you have enough deductions that you would have owed no tax had you filed in a timely way. This could eliminate not only the tax you owe, but also the interest on that tax.

By way of review, you're not finished. Let's say you still owe a significant amount of tax and interest from that unfilled year, and you managed to get that one-time penalty abatement granted.

If paying the revised amount due is a current hardship, *then ask for a payment plan!*

The IRS will notify you that you have a tax due. Then they will make a formal, written demand for full payment. They'll advise you to contact them within thirty or forty-five days to make arrangements in the event you don't simply write them a check and mail the money in.

If they hear nothing from you (which is a very bad strategy on your part), their tactics will become more aggressive. They could place a lien on your assets. These include your home, if you own it, and the title to your car, especially if it is free and clear. It is common for them to seize the money in your bank account.

Any tangible assets you own can be seized and sold to satisfy your tax debts.

Additionally, they can and usually will seize a portion of your earnings. This is called a *wage garnishment.*

If you are in a DIY mode, you need to phone the IRS immediately, or visit one of their field offices, to make arrangements so that they'll promptly release the liens. Typically they'll insist on making a payment plan with you.

You can have a tax firm intercede on your behalf and negotiate the release of liens. People often feel comfortable doing this because experiencing the trauma of a sudden seizure or freezing of assets can be emotionally debilitating. It's like being hit in the solar plexus, many say.

The tax firm will usually require some sort of upfront payment for its services. Almost always, they're going to ask you for more than they'll accept.

So they may start with $2000 to get a lien released and arrange a payment plan. Try to get them down to $500. If they are doing any volume of business, they can still make a profit on getting most liens released at this lower fee.

Then ask them for a payment plan on any overall amount they have agreed to.

Lien releases are typically urgent transactions. They need to be done as fast as possible, because you need your paycheck and access to your bank balances. A lien on your house may involve a slower pace. That will hang like a cloud, perhaps for several years, until you want to sell or refinance. Once your loan or sale transaction is in escrow, to remove that cloud on the title, the escrow company will compel you to pay off the IRS as a condition of allowing the escrow to close and the sale to be officially consummated.

I mentioned that it *is* a possibility to stiff the tax-resolution company. They are not dummies, so they will try to structure their work so they *are* paid, completely, even if you are on a monthly plan with them. But in some cases, their work is unavoidably front-loaded, meaning they do it all at once, at the beginning of their relationship with you.

Arranging a lien release or a simple payment plan is like this. They might need a few to several billable hours to complete these tasks, but you'll be paying for six months or more.

Once their actual work is done, if you can no longer afford to pay them in addition to retiring your tax debt, then you will obviously have to make a choice about forking over more money to that firm.

Very few will send your account to collections or sue you in small-claims court if they have seen enough dough to retire their actual expenditure of time. Plus, many these days are afraid that you'll beef about them to the Better Business Bureau, or to Yelp, or to Ripoff Report—or to all three!

It is important to remember this regarding ALL kinds of debts: as I said in a prior chapter, *you might decide to file for bankruptcy to wipe them out.*

So not only is there a sequence of strategies and statuses to seek when doing a tax-relief program with the IRS, there is a sequence of strategies to employ that could eventuate in the nuclear option—a Chapter 7 filing.

Once you have filed, a tax-resolution provider has no more claim to repayment than a credit-card company. It will achieve no preferred treatment from the bankruptcy trustee who oversees your case.

It makes sense, therefore, to stretch out your payments to a tax-resolution company, as it does to any creditor, if you believe that bankruptcy is your endgame solution.

Like the Grim Reaper, from whom no one escapes, a bankruptcy filing and discharge (about six months after filing) will undo 99% of your debts.

I know I treat this topic in its own chapter, but I am specifically discussing crossover strategies with you now.

At this writing, there are two significant types of debts that are not generally discharged in bankruptcy: (1) spousal and child support and (2) IRS tax debts.

Number one is attributable to society's interest in protecting the interests of the vulnerable. But number two is worth some discussion.

We've all heard that death and taxes are unavoidable. Not so fast! You might be allowed to nix your IRS tax debt in bankruptcy.

There are some exceptions, but the general rule is if your tax debts are more than three years old, you can seek their discharge in a Chapter 7 bankruptcy.

Consider this scenario. You owe $150,000 to the IRS from debts that are three years old and older. Suddenly you're out of work, and you cannot continue to make your monthly payments of $3000 plus interest.

Providing you pass the means test for income and assets under the bankruptcy code, you might be able not only to stop those payments but also to get that entire IRS debt obligation off your back.

What if some of the debt is less than three years old and the remainder is old enough to qualify?

You have a strategic choice to make. You can wait to file your bankruptcy until ALL of the debt is 36 or more months older. Or, you can file now, asking that the 36-month-old debt be discharged, while accepting that the remaining balance will have to be paid off.

Then you'll need to arrange a suitable payment plan with the IRS to put this into place.

Remember this as a cautionary note: the IRS is the biggest collections agency on earth. So don't expect them to cut you that much slack once you have discharged a substantial amount of tax debt.

At the same time, they are obligated to treat you fairly. So the entire spectrum of tax resolutions within their power will still be available to you. You'll qualify pretty much automatically for SOME payment plan based on your postdischarge income and expenses.

You may also qualify for CNC if your income is equal to or lower than your documented expenses. And I would not rule out an offer in compromise either.

Remember, *don't under any circumstances challenge the right of the IRS to collect taxes*. Go to www.irs.gov and look up the article "The Truth about Frivolous Tax Arguments," which the IRS occasionally updates. That will set you straight about their antipathy toward tax protesters. Here's what *Newsweek* magazine said on February 5, 2018:

> *The people who advance such baseless arguments are commonly known as "tax protesters" or "tax deniers." Again, they always lose when they advance these arguments in court. Some are so adamant about their quixotic arguments, however, that they all but volunteer to*

go to prison rather than admit that they do not have a leg to stand on.

As with most transactions in life, you'll get more of what you want with honey than with vinegar. And there's no reason to express a radical viewpoint or to politicize your tax debts.

The objective is not to win an argument. The objective is to dramatically reduce or entirely wipe out your tax obligation.

As you've seen in this chapter, there are viable and perfectly lawful means for doing that.

Chapter 5

Student-Loan Forgiveness

Y<small>ou</small> may have heard the statistics: Americans owe over $1.5 trillion in student-loan debt. Approximately 44 million borrowers share this burden.

The average graduate of the class of 2016 had $37,172 in student-loan debt. This was up 6% from the prior year. Averages mean that some borrowers are on the hook for zero or merely a few thousand bucks, while others, especially those that have gone on to graduate study, can owe $250,000.

The total student-loan debt outstanding is roughly $620 billion more than the total U.S. credit-card debt. This is staggering.

Compounding the amount of the debt is the fact that millions of borrowers are in default. It isn't hard to figure out why.

At the risk of making you weary of statistics, approximately 40% of Americans are doing work that is beneath them. They're overeducated and underpaid. Just making ends meet is hard enough, but if you're carrying $100K in student loans, then the standard payment on those runs about 1% a month, or $1000.

That's $12,000 a year. If you are stuck in a poorly paid McJob where you earn $12 per hour, then you're earning merely $24,000 working over the course of 50 weeks.

There's tax withholding, and you probably have some costs that also bring down the amount of take-home pay you can call your own.

Let's say you're netting $18,000 after taxes and other costs. How can you pay back $1000 each and every month when you're only seeing $1500 in total?

Can anyone these days live on a mere $500 a month? Even if you're staying on a friend's couch or living in your parents' basement, you have to get around, right?

Where is that car payment coming from, and car insurance? Are you going to live naked?

You get my point. For millions, even simply servicing the loan payments is beyond their means. And if they're unemployed, well, forget about it. No way can they pay!

This is why a huge number of student-loan borrowers are in default. They have stopped making payments, and they're nine or more months in arrears.

Here is the breakdown for defaults in 2017, according to *Forbes* magazine (October 6, 2017):

- Total default rate: 11.5% (previous: 11.3%)
- Total number of borrowers who defaulted in the last three years: 580,671

- Time period measured: October 1, 2013–September 30, 2016
- Public-college student-loan default rate: 11.3% (previous: 11.3%)
- Private-college student-loan default rate: 7.4% (previous: 7.0%)
- For-profit-college student-loan default rate: 15.5% (previous: 15.0%)

These stats don't capture the number of borrowers on the edge, the ones that are scraping by, making their payments but about to stop, as well as those that are late, but not technically in default, which is declared at the ninth month of tardiness.

It has been widely reported that home ownership is declining because of the student-loan mess that we're in. The amount of disposable income available even to those that are paying on time is severely limited, so they cannot qualify for mortgages. Nor do they have enough net spending power to handle mortgage payments plus property taxes, insurance, and anticipated repairs and maintenance.

Plus, few can afford to put together a down payment. In many cases they can't turn to relatives or to parents, because these folks are also repaying their loans!

Why did so many people borrow so much and get stuck with an overwhelming burden?

There is a widespread belief that college graduates earn far more than those with high-school educations alone.

At one time this may have been true. But in the United States, real, inflation-adjusted wages haven't risen for thirty-five years. With more grads chasing fewer well-paying jobs, and with downsizing, automation, outsourcing, and offshoring, the jobs that remain simply do not pay as much as they did for baby-boomers.

To borrow a crass phrase, college grads are a dime a dozen, especially those that are not majoring in STEM (science, technology, engineering, and math) subjects or are not computer programmers.

If you asked many people the stark question, "If you could do it over, would you go to college or at least finance it through student loans?" many would say no.

I have five earned degrees, so you would be correct to infer that I love learning. So I'm glad I took out and duly paid back my student loans.

But that was back in the day when I could take up to eighteen semester units at junior college for only $7.50! Yes, that is not a misprint: for seven dollars and fifty cents I could take a dozen and a half units, six full classes worth.

Why did I need loans if school was so cheap? Books, believe it or not, cost disproportionately more than tuition, and I had to pay rent and other living costs. Federal student loans enabled me to scrape by, to put gas in my very used VW, and commute to my job.

I transferred to a state university, where tuition was substantially higher, earning my first two degrees, a BA and an MA.

My remaining three degrees, a PhD, a JD, and an

MBA, were all done at pricey private universities. By that time I was teaching and getting scholarships. After I got my doctorate and started a lucrative consulting practice, I paid for my law degree and MBA out of pocket, incurring zero debt.

Student loans gave me my start, and I'm grateful I had them.

But times have changed, and the social compact has changed. This is the unwritten code that said, if you graduate from college you'd be able to afford a middle-class lifestyle. This notion included the implied promise that you'd easily retire your student-loan debts, because you'd be earning plenty of dough.

The marriage, three kids, picket fence, two cars in the garage, and nice vacations every year would all be yours, if you wanted them.

Sadly, I do not need to elaborate on how that vision seems cruelly quaint as I write these words.

I worked my way through college full-time while studying full-time. As investment genius John Bogle said about his youth, "I grew up with the priceless advantage of having to work for what I got." (Though it didn't feel like an advantage at the time, I can tell you!)

But as I look back, I can see that my education was effectively FREE. Certainly at the junior-college level it was a bargain, and it was even a very good value at the state-college level, where I earned those first two degrees. But after that, because I had skills and sheepskins, I was able to more or less navigate my way with the wind at my back.

If you choose to not pay back your loans, or if you simply cannot pay them back, you are simply going to be yielding to a new reality, one that didn't apply so much in my day.

Good jobs are few. Incomes are down, and so is disposable pay. Student-loan debt levels are through the roof as well.

I should also note that college costs are out of whack. They have vastly outpaced inflation.

My law-school tuition cost a grand total of $48,000 at a very selective private school. The same degree will set back today's students about $200,000.

And starting salaries have actually gone down for many attorneys. The job market for lawyers has almost collapsed, and wages are a fraction of what they were when I graduated.

If my investment in law school merely kept up with inflation, it would cost a recent, 2017 graduate only $104,876. Why are current students required to pay an $96,000 on top of the inflation-adjusted amount?

The short answer is runaway administrative costs.

Unlike businesses, which strive for greater efficiencies over time, until very recently colleges and professional schools had not encountered pressures to cut costs.

To put it simply, schooling ended up being far too expensive for no good reason.

Should you have to repay what you borrowed plus interest for twenty or thirty years because schools couldn't manage to rein in costs?

The upshot is, it isn't your fault that you're up to your earlobes in student-loan debt. And you are certainly not to blame for having inadequate funds to pay off your loans.

Let's turn now to what you can do to reduce and eliminate this burden. Happily, there is a way to pay back ZERO DOLLARS on your student loans, even if you owe $250,000.

Public loan forgiveness is one of your options for repayment. The Public Service Loan Forgiveness (PSLF) program forgives the remaining balance on your direct loans after you have made 120 qualifying monthly payments under a qualifying repayment plan while working full-time for a qualifying employer.

This may not seem terribly attractive, but if you compare it to the typical term of a student loan payback period, twenty to thirty years, then ten years looks like a walk in the park.

Who can take advantage of this? Typically, public-school teachers, police officers, and those that work in government can benefit. In theory, if you work full-time for a nonprofit organization, such as the American Heart Association, you may be eligible.

However, I want to caution you. Under the Trump administration it has become more difficult to qualify.

So you need to fill in the appropriate forms and make sure everything is shipshape before you can assume you'll qualify.

Other programs are available to practically everyone, especially income-based repayment plans. These schemes enable you to bypass the standard repayment, which can take a bite out of your income (if you have one). And without an income, or if you are unemployed or only casually working every now and then, standard payments can be overwhelming.

There are a few critical variables in qualifying for income-based repayment plans. One, of course, is your gross income. Are you making $25,000 per year or less? I can tell you right away you may qualify for a ZERO-DOLLAR PAYMENT at that income level. (Interest continues to accrue on the unpaid balance. However, if you achieve loan forgiveness after a number of years, the principal and interest will be discharged.)

Another thing that affects the repayment amount is the number of your dependents. If you are a single person with no kids to support, then at a $25,000 income, you'd probably get that zero-dollar repayment.

This could be far less than you'd pay the standard way, depending on your level of student-loan debt. If you owe $100,000 and your standard payment would be $1000 per month, being single, with a $25,000 income, you'll in all likelihood pay zero dollars.

But if your income is, say, $35,000, you'll have to pay something.

At this rate of pay, that amount could jump to $200 per month, but that's a heck of a lot better than paying a grand every thirty days, correct?

What if you're married and your spouse earns significantly more than you do? If you file separately, you may still qualify for a reduced or zero-dollar payment. However, if you file jointly, then your incomes will be pooled for qualification purposes.

In this case, you may not do any better than your current commitment to making the standard payment.

Let's change the equation. What if you are single with three dependents, including yourself? Then that $35,000 income might not disqualify you from having a dramatically reduced or zero-dollar payment.

Another variable that's factored into the repayment equation is the state in which you reside. Everyone knows the cost of living in places like New York and California is higher than in, say, Michigan or Colorado.

The repayment tables are adjusted based on how far your income stretches where you live. The weight of place of residence isn't heavy overall, but it does inform what you'll be on the hook for.

Now one thing you absolutely need to know is this: if you qualify right now for a zero-dollar payment, this is great. But it is based either on current monthly income or on your income level as stated on last year's official tax return.

Sometimes you can elect to use the number more favorable to you. Let's say last year you reported an income of $25,000. But you've just found out you're getting a raise to $30,000, effective next month.

What then? Do you have to use the $30,000 figure?

In my opinion, no: until that raise occurs, it is a mere expectancy and not a sure thing. Sorry to spoil the party, but any number of things can happen between now and then. Your company could go broke. You might move or become disabled. I could go on with this parade of potential horrible events, but you get the point.

My favorite quote from the financial firm Dun & Bradstreet says, "The deal isn't made until the money is paid!" So what do you do? You can submit the prior six months of your check stubs as proof of income, or you can probably go with submitting a copy of last year's tax return.

Select the income source that will characterize your financial resources in the light that is most favorable to you in order to qualify for a maximal reduction in loan payments.

You need to know something else that is vital about reducing your student-loan payments under loan-forgiveness programs:

You must requalify each and every year.

You can't get a repayment schedule of zero dollars a month for thirty years right now, and forget about it. Every year you'll need to submit proof of income. Then a recalculation will be performed and sent to you, telling you what your adjusted repayment amount will be for the coming twelve months.

There is a slight cost-of-living adjustment made year to year. So if last year your income was $25,000 on the nose, but this year it is $25,400, in all likelihood there will be no upward adjustment made.

But if you won the lottery (good for you!) or you got a big promotion and you're earning $50,000 per year, expect to be dinged.

Of course that extra payout may not last either. You could lose your cushy job to a robot. For the purposes of student-loan repayment, that's a good thing, because you'll probably requalify for a zero-dollar monthly obligation.

OK, so far, so good: I've addressed reduced and zero-dollar payments. But what is this term loan forgiveness all about?

Let's say your income is depressed and you get that zero-dollar payment. You're set up on a thirty-year repayment program. If your current circumstances don't change, for example if you are disabled and unable to work, then you will qualify for that zero payment year after year.

In thirty years, the principal amount you owe, plus accruing interest, will seem huge. You borrowed $100,000, but now that debt amounts to $200,000 or more. Will the collectors come a-calling and force you to repay that tab?

As the forgiveness program stands today, the answer is "absolutely not." You played by the rules, and now the government will forgive your remaining loan balance, no matter what it is.

It could be $1 or it could be $250,000. It is wiped out, gone, done with, in the rearview mirror.

The same principle applies to the end result if your income gyrated like crazy during those thirty years. As long as you kept up with your payments, when you had them, you will qualify for balance forgiveness at the end of the rainbow.

I know what some of you are thinking: "Do you know how old I'll be at the end of thirty years?" You'll be the exact age you'll be if you *don't* participate in these loan-forgiveness programs!

But you will have paid back a lot more money.

There are some tricks involved in the process. You'll want to fully review the pertinent student-loan websites hosted by the government. One of them is www .studentaid.com. There you'll learn all about the various programs available, including public-service loan forgiveness.

You can sign up for loan forgiveness on your own, providing you're patient and careful. It doesn't have to cost you anything.

However, you should know that there is work involved, and you may want to look into getting professional help from a firm specializing in doing paperwork for former students such as yourself.

Their fees are all over the map. I know of some firms that charge a flat $495. That is to do the first year's paperwork. After that, you're on your own to requalify and to document your income to the government, or they'll negotiate a separate fee to do this for you.

There are other firms that will charge a first-time fee, say $495, plus, after your paperwork has been approved by the government, they'll ding you for a "maintenance fee" of $39 a month.

What are you getting for the money? They'll take responsibility for submitting the annual paperwork on your behalf.

If you do the math, they're making out like bandits. $39 a month for 29 years amounts to an additional $468 per year—times 29. That's $13,572; plus you have paid $495 for the startup.

That totals $14,067!

Wait a minute. If you owe $150,000 and they say they are going to save you $75,000 of that, then $14,535 sounds reasonable, doesn't it?

That's how they sell it, and they're smart to do it that way. But remember, you can sign up for free at a government website and not pay the initial fee, and you can requalify annually for free as well.

So what's the good part?

If you're very busy right now, the $495 deal without the monthly commitment may be a bargain, at least for you.

In any case, you need to be cautious about having a for-profit company assist you. If you want to exploit them for informational purposes and get them to do some initial calculations for you, then this makes a lot of sense.

If you call them, they'll ask you for a lot of information, including your Social Security number. You do not have to give it to them unless and until you decide to have them do your paperwork for you.

Tell them how much you owe, your state of residence, your number of dependents, your income, your total federal loan amount, and the approximate loan-origination years. With that information alone, they should be able to disclose what your payment would be under current programs.

Compare what they say to your standard repayment. If it is substantially less, then go forth to a government site and start the paperwork.

If the difference is fractional, say your payment is currently stated at $100 and they say you'll qualify for $85 a month, then, when you total in their costs, it may not be worth it to use them or to even bother doing it yourself.

Chapter 6

Why Try to Repay?

There is a huge industry dedicated to helping you to TRY to pay down your debts. Making an effort seems noble, as in "It's the LEAST I can do!"

But should you even try?

Have you ever taken a good long look at a picture of billionaire capitalist Sir Richard Branson?

Tanned, athletic, typically just back from a hot-air balloon adventure or some other diversion, he always looks tremendously toothy, robust, and pinch-me-happy.

What's his secret? I ask you.

"He's *rich*, filthy *rich*!" you could reply with certitude.

That is true. Having a billion or more bucks or euros does qualify as rich. But I say you're mistaking effect for cause.

My take on his almost too-giddy-to-be-true approach to life is that he's rich *because he's happy* more than the other way around.

His wealth and exuberance are flowing from what I call NOT TRYING.

I'll lay out the difference between Sir Richard and typical knaves like you, up to their eyeballs in debt, who don't get rich or enjoy life to the fullest.

If you're like most folks, you're trying too hard, toiling to exhaustion, stressing yourself to the max in pursuit of life's goodies.

In so doing, you're missing both the fun *and* the money.

Do you know why so many of us love these book titles: *The Lazy Man's Way to Riches* and *The Four-Hour Workweek*? The titles don't promise a gold watch and a cozy retirement in a banana republic in old age, but a comfortable, cozy, natural pace in achieving the good things in life *now*, when we're vibrant enough to really enjoy them.

Who wants to jog along a tropical beach worrying about his pacemaker and titanium hip replacements? Yet that's the *best* you're probably going to get if you take the conventional path to success, as it is promoted in the U.S. and a number of other consumption-driven countries.

We are sold a bill of goods telling us that it is through effort—unrelenting, nose-to-the-grindstone exertion—that is responsible for our greatest achievements. Not so.

One book of recent vintage says it takes 10,000 hours to develop mastery of anything. Baloney.

Do you think the mighty Babe Ruth put in 10,000 hours as a kid fielding, pitching, and hitting baseballs? Even if he did later on, it was in service to his natural ability. Springing from that fount, it made sense and felt right to him.

Our mistake is believing that if we put in 10,000 or 50,000 hours doing something, we'll learn to hit a record number of home runs or become crackerjack bridge players or spellbinding public speakers. That's preposterous.

Well-placed effort is one thing. But most of us are hypnotized and goaded into sinking tremendous efforts into areas of low-yield results. Especially when we take tips from others, poorly placed efforts are what we are doomed to make, which consigns us to unproductive, unhappy, and unhealthy lives.

I know a law-school graduate who sat for the infamous California state bar exam a dozen times. She invested six years after graduating from law school, putting her professional and personal life on hold, while studying for, taking, and retaking that devilishly hard test every six months.

Her marriage was stressed; her finances were strained. She declined countless invitations to parties and barbecues and evenings out and vacations and the normal occasions of life while chained to this cycle of failure.

Why did she do this? She liked the *idea* of being a lawyer. It held high social status for her, and perhaps her family thought it would be nice to have an attorney in the fold. All the wrong reasons, by the way.

She interpreted the fact that learning the law was difficult as a sign that it was especially worthwhile. In point of fact, the fact that it required Herculean effort on her part to study and retain the material should have sent her the opposite message.

It wasn't right for her. She didn't have the aptitude for it. The fact that it was such drudgery should have presaged that once she was licensed, actually practicing wouldn't be a dreamy cakewalk.

She did go on to practice, successfully, but her career was derailed, and she quit as a result of the unrelenting stress she experienced in feeling inadequate to the task.

If you are overexerting yourself in pursuit of a goal, such as paying off your debts, you should do a calibration check. By this, I mean ask yourself: is this really right for me?

Or am I straining because this vocation or job or activity or feeling of commitment is fundamentally going against my nature, or my gifts, or everyday enjoyments?

If repaying debts requires Herculean effort and you are hopelessly ball-and-chaining your life because of it, you're making a mistake by trying.

As a teenager, I liked being a busboy in a restaurant. The servers were nice to me, and I got to eat two meals on the house—whatever I wanted. Then I scooped ice cream at a parlor, which was a step up in status, but I hated it. Why? I can't really tell you.

Maybe it was being watched as I worked by impatient customers who were vibing me to give them an extra dollop. Anyway, I quit the second place in short order.

And that's the right thing to do with misfits: abandon them before they ensnare you.

This happens when connecting with people too. When I was dating and mating, there were people who seemed to have tremendous interpersonal résumés. They were nice, well-spoken, easygoing, and similar to me in certain ways, but the parts never added up to a whole package.

Something was missing.

"How's Pam?" my dad would ask.

"I don't know, Dad, how is she?" I would wisecrack. This was years after high school and she had gone her way and I'd gone mine.

Adorable as she was to Dad, she wasn't right for me, and I wasn't right for her. All of the effort in the world wasn't going to substitute for that absent spark or connection or whatever we could call it. And you can't quite explain the absence of interpersonal chemistry, though we do recognize know its presence when we hit it off with someone.

A big clue is that being with them is EFFORT-LESS. There is no TRY required.

In a vintage Woody Allen movie, some happy elderly couples are commenting about how they knew their eventual life partners were "the one." A sweet granny type says, "You can always tell when it's a good melon." Another one says, "There's a lid for every pot." I've taken up cooking, and she's right. You know when the lid fits, and you know when it doesn't.

Maybe you can still cook a meal with an ill-fitting lid, but something in the experience is sacrificed. I wouldn't want to make a habit of it.

If you're working too hard at something, including an attempt to restore financial stability, typically something is wrong.

In the fun and instructive movie *The Karate Kid*, Mr. Miyagi, the wise elder who is teaching young Daniel various self-defense moves, makes a crucial correction.

Daniel is straining too much, and Miyagi says: "There is no TRY in karate."

Bruce Lee, the world-renowned martial artist and movie star, said the same thing, but he elaborated on it. Let's say you're throwing a punch. *Your speed and impact increases as your effort decreases*, not the other way around.

Our intuition is absolutely wrong, because we equate more effort with more results.

Lee explained that one set of muscles propels your strike in the intended direction, and this is natural and good. But if we "effort" it, straining as we thrust, a second set of muscles will engage, and this slows down the first set.

It's like having one foot on the gas and the other on the brake. One reduces the efficiency of the other and creates drag.

Imagine driving your car in a vacuum, where there is no wind resistance to your forward motion. You'd reach incredible acceleration.

This is what NOT TRYING accomplishes.

I recall reading an unconventional book on self-management. It said if you can't get your job done during a normal workday or workweek, you're doing it wrong; you're inefficient. That resonated for me.

When I came out of law school and (fortunately!) passed the bar exam on the first try, I interviewed for some jobs. At that point I was already a successful management consultant, earning in the six figures, and I liked my profession.

I got a few offers to change vocations and to practice law, but they seemed to entail far too much work and stress for the amount of money I was already pulling in on my own.

Moreover, the working day was superlong, because one was expected to log twelve hours routinely. "There's something wrong with this picture!" I murmured to myself.

And there is. If you have to put in 150% of the time to earn 150% of the average pay, that's not my definition of productivity. Putting in 50% to earn 150%—well, that would be more like it. That way you can get ahead, socking away some funds while still having time to enjoy other aspects of life.

Try less and get more is a far better prescription for health, wealth, and happiness than *work twice as long and hard and earn more.*

A relative of mine had a tough childhood. He dropped out of high school because his dad died at a young age, so as a teen he had to work to support himself and his mom.

He overcame a speech impediment to become a successful door-to-door salesman. He prospered and opened his own business and finance company. Wearing custom-made suits and snazzy shoes, he had everything, including a yacht at the marina.

Then, at thirty-eight, he had a heart attack.

This changed his outlook. He went from being a Type-A, take-no-prisoners, hard-bitten businessman to becoming a Zenlike sage. He expressed his new philosophy in two simple words:

WHY BOTHER?

He had been living in the middle of busy Beverly Hills, California, where sirens interrupted his sleep, so he moved to the Monterey Peninsula, next to the ocean and golf courses and a stone's throw from the famed Seventeen-Mile Drive.

Could he afford this? Not really, but he figured he needed the fresh air and healthy atmosphere, and if he didn't make big changes in his lifestyle, he'd be dead.

Above all, he decided to work less and to take his leaden foot off the gas.

The funny thing is that he became more productive, and his new business—one that didn't depend on a big office and staff—really started to prosper.

"Why bother?" became his merry mantra, which he repeated to me with the giddiness of a yogi who had discovered levitation.

And that phrase pretty well captures some of what I'm saying here about repaying onerous debts.

WHY TRY?

Trying implies resistance and friction, and these elements inhibit progress.

By the way, that relative of mine is alive and kicking in his nineties. *Not trying* has worked out very, very well for him.

This isn't to say you can't burn the candle at both ends at least for a time.

I was in sales management with Time-Life Books at age nineteen. I was responsible for a staff that worked three four-hour shifts. Plus, I went to college full-time.

This was before online learning, so I actually had to commute to campus, which fortunately was only fifteen minutes from work. My stress levels were off the charts.

"How can a nineteen-year-old have high blood pressure?" my physician asked. I outlined my schedule and he simply nodded.

As I said, you can do things like this at a certain age and stage, at least briefly. But do them on a sustained basis, and you'll burn out.

Later, as a management consultant, I spent Monday through Friday in distant cities and hamlets, flying home for weekends. The stresses of my projects were substantial in themselves. But add the rigors of long-distance commuting, and the effects were cumulative, and staggering.

It got to a point where I didn't take my own car to the airport on Sunday afternoons. I used rental cars in my home city as well as on the road. They were easier and faster to pick up and return instead of parking my own ride.

When my consulting morphed into gigantic projects, I tried to handle most of the details by myself. Worrying that others would add needless administration, I didn't delegate.

That was dumb. I should have invoked a "Why try?" philosophy. This would have enabled me to curtail my presence while letting others help me out.

Finally, having what I considered enough money in the bank, I simply caught a plane home at one point and stayed off the tarmac and out of hotels for years.

The stress, rich foods, constant jet lag, strange beds, and other incidents of travel had taken their toll. I ended up with a zillion frequent-flyer miles, yet the last thing I wanted to do was to board another plane to take a vacation. I'd break into a macabre laugh at the mere mention of traveling again.

This sounds ironic, but we see something similar with people who are waiting for retirement. I know a fellow who can't wait to retire from his job with a city water department. He only has another thirteen years to go!

And he's miserable. Typically, people who postpone their fun until retirement get so burnt out, so physically damaged and stressed, that retirement doesn't seem that enjoyable when it rolls around.

That's if they survive long enough to make old bones, as my mom would say.

The common thread between my incessant traveling for business and my friend's countdown to retirement is that both postures require expending huge efforts.

Waiting for time to pass in a dull post isn't much fun.

And even leasing a suite by the month at the Four Seasons Hotel in Houston can get old.

If you're trying too hard, something is wrong. And you'll run aground before long.

I realize what I'm saying belies the work ethic that many of us have been raised to follow. This is the idea that there is something redeeming in laboring long and hard to achieve a result. That good things result from the sweat of our brows.

If you have no other options, then work away, that's what I say. When I was out on my own for the first time and squeaking by on a tiny income, going to college, I had to take the work I could get. And I couldn't come across to my employers as an ungrateful slacker.

The appearance of "trying really hard" was part of the performance required of me. Just as "seeming to really care" is a prerequisite to doing customer-service work, when you're new to the labor market, you need to appear eager and committed and willing to go that extra mile.

And as I've said elsewhere in this book, appearing to *want* to pay your bills is good theater. You can earn a certain amount of relief from creditors such as the tax authorities when you want to "do the right thing." It rings the right bell for them, making them more pliable.

Just as babies mature into toddlers, and teens into adults, we must mature into a proper understanding of the relationship between efforts and results. At first, they are positively correlated, especially in a workplace where we don't know anything.

Trying and learning go hand in hand. But once you know the basics, you can usher in improvements—short-cuts and efficiencies. Even baggers at supermarkets learn to herd shopping carts in the parking lot instead of fetching and returning to the store with them one or two at a time.

The history of human progress is all about realizing efficiencies and benefiting from them. My primitive typing skills are made irrelevant by the ability of this computer program to erase and to spell-check my scribbling. I can concentrate on my message and not on how it appears on the page.

But *shouldn't* I learn to type? That train left the station long ago, and anyway my hunting-and-pecking style isn't all that slow.

Yet that notion "I *should* do this better" gets us into trouble. Early in my schooling I did well in math, and I have the report cards to prove it! But in high school, I tanked in this topic. You can blame my teachers, or my attention span; it doesn't much matter.

Facts are facts. I excelled at other topics, though, acing them easily. "Why such low marks in math?" my parents inquired.

I couldn't offer a satisfactory explanation. It was as if my A's were all but invisible, that I had genuine strengths as well that were not reflected on those progress reports.

Management sage Peter F. Drucker, who was my MBA professor for two and a half years, said we waste too much time shoring up weaknesses instead of promoting our strengths.

He cites the example of Mozart, the musical prodigy.

"We wouldn't want Mozart wasting a moment on math given his musical gifts," Drucker emphatically pointed out. But he went on to say that the school system errs by doing this, because it focuses students on remedying weaknesses.

This misplaced focus retards the development of areas in which the students have demonstrated their strengths.

If Mozart pined away, thinking, "I should be better at math," that would have been precious time he could have channeled into making more immortal music.

I think it is fairly sure that Mozart composed with great ease, that beautiful melodies flowed through his consciousness easily, friction-free. This is exactly how "work" and almost every human endeavor should operate.

There is no "try" in music, or in karate, or in becoming unchained from debt, or in anything else. That is, if you're proceeding properly and that activity is genuinely for you.

You've shown some flaws by incurring debt that is very difficult if not impossible to repay. Maybe you're just terrible at budgeting, or you have a low aptitude for earning, but you're a whiz at spending!

Millions upon millions are just like you, so why obsess over a weakness? You could be refocusing on your strengths.

I'm a writer largely because I sit at my keyboard and the words flow through me. What wants and needs to be articulated comes forth in torrents and not in trickles.

(For instance, I had no idea I would use that alliteration of T words at the end of the last sentence until it cascaded out of my mind.)

Unlike many who struggle, I am a writer because I DON'T work at it. It comes to me, just as a natural swing comes to a pro baseball player.

Along this line, I am a big believer in beginner's luck. As you know, this is the instant success that some experience with a new activity. The first time I went bowling, on my first toss, I bowled a strike. I did not go on to become a champion in this sport. But my precociousness augured well for that.

I've seen this time and again. In areas where I've had instant success, I've gone on to become very, very skilled. This is partly attributable to reinforcement. We tend to repeat what is rewarded.

But I believe so-called beginner's luck runs deeper than that. When at first we succeed, it is a signal of talent, or at least of a predisposition to succeed in that area with minimal cultivation.

When I have an hour to kill, I hit a bucket of balls with a pal in Pebble Beach. I'm no golfer. (Well, that's not totally true. I'm a decent *miniature* golfer!) But on this occasion, we teed off with no purpose in mind. I had never driven a golf ball before, putting a big swing on it. But when I did, apparently it was impressive, flying far and straight.

My pal joked that I had played before and I was hustling him.

"Not true!" I insisted.

The same thing happened when I played some tennis against my sister. My serves were mostly "aces," powerful and true. She swore that I had played before, which I really hadn't.

Now I play tennis frequently, and I'm surely less impressive than I was playing her!

The point is that we have proclivities for achieving in certain ways. I *was* a very good baseball player, and I had a good swing. There's no assurance that that skill can translate into a good golf or tennis stroke. But we can say the athletic potential is there.

If tennis is for me, I shouldn't have to labor at it, toiling away without a feeling of reward. On the contrary, I should experience some victories early in my development.

If I'm struggling, something is terribly wrong. And masters of the game aren't likely to console me with the words, "Don't worry—everyone stinks at first," because that's not true.

I've seen peewees on the court who are no more than three or four, and they already show promise.

Talent and skill trump effort and hard work.

I wrote a book that was inspired by my dad's career called *How To Sell Like a Natural Born Salesperson*. In it, I outline many of the differences between naturals and those who have to work at this occupation.

Naturals, among other things, do have the gift of gab. They communicate easily. They are understood. They are almost inherently persuasive and, some would say, both charming and disarming.

If you are by nature an introvert—you shy away from people and don't gladly socialize—selling is probably not for you. As with anything, there are exceptions.

You can teach yourself to sell. You can force yourself to make cold calls, just as introverts can cross that wide, slippery floor and invite someone to dance with them.

But it's hard to do. Even if you succeed now, you might revert to nonselling tendencies enough without constant prodding.

That's no way to live, because with each success you're also feeling, "This isn't me."

Shells aren't just for coming out of—they are there to crawl back into if we find the outside inhospitable.

If you have accomplished something *only* from hard work and unrelenting grit, you may feel a temporary victory and a surge of self-satisfaction. I should point out that some people climb mountains purely for the challenge.

However, if you are like most, the satisfaction from achieving an ultimate victory will be insufficient to motivate you to repeat the process. More likely, you'll be "one and done."

When it comes to debt repayment, you'll move heaven and earth to make payments while not putting a dent in the size of the debt. Despite your gargantuan efforts, the mountain you're climbing will seem the same height, if not even more difficult to scale.

And if you're like me, you'll feel stupid for trying. The odds were stacked against you when you started the steep climb out of debt. So why did you undertake the ascent to begin with?

I was doing my PhD at USC and teaching part-time at Cal State Northridge. I didn't have enough spending money, so I looked at the job board in the career office.

Spotting a part-time opportunity at a nearby office-supply firm, I interviewed and was hired.

Following their script to the letter, I made my first call and sold the first person I spoke to. He was a baker; I'll never forget it.

Instantly the sales manager beamed, "He's a master! He's a master!"

Which was true. If it was not totally manifested then, it became apparent to all a few years later after I'd written books and consulted on the subject. My instant success was attributable in part to my prior sales victories, but selling their products at that time, on a full commission basis, was utterly new to me.

Yet I hit the jackpot on the first try.

This isn't unusual if you are doing what you were made to do.

At the same time, if you are uncomfortable with something or someone from the get-go, then *let go*!

Activities, tasks, and jobs that you find offensive are clear-cut invitations to flee.

But what if you are *kind of* good at something, OK at it, not great, but adequate? This can be problematic.

Also challenging is the person that finds he or she is "great at everything." This looks like a blessing, but it can be a curse.

Here's what I mean. Let's say you have tried lots of things but have succeeded at only one of them. Well, your path is clearly in front of you. Go with that one identified strength.

I know an entrepreneur who had very little formal education. He has started several successful businesses and lives well.

Asked why he became an entrepreneur, he replied, "I had no choice. Nobody else would hire me without an education." As he saw it, necessity created his strength.

No problem. But there is a challenge if you are pulled in lots of directions where you have experienced partial or early success.

I became a very good student later in life. I learned how to learn, so undertaking and completing degrees became, not totally easy for me, but let's say, comfortable.

After earning my PhD and two degrees before that, I enrolled in law school. The official reason was to protect my intellectual properties, my books, and my new sales and service innovations.

Unofficially, it was a mountain to climb, and it represented some unfinished family business. My granddad and dad came close to becoming licensed attorneys, but never crossed the finishing line.

With my PhD done, earning a good living as a consultant, I decided to write the checks for law school and attend part-time. It was harder than I imagined. But my pride was on the line, and I persevered, graduated early, and took the bar exam early. I passed it on the first try, as I mentioned.

I'm largely glad I did this because I was freed from the need to do it. I hope that makes sense.

I answered the big what-if question that had vexed my forebears: what if I were an attorney? With license in hand, I *was* one, so that freed me to practice or not practice as I wished.

To look back, was this worth all of the investment, effort, and the forgone income that I would have made had I *not* gone to law school? Yes and no.

I was so good at studying and completing degrees once I undertook them that finishing the law degree was simply a given—it was taken for granted.

But it wasn't easy, which for me was a trap. I relished the challenge and told myself, "Look, you're a PhD, at the top of the intellectual food chain, surely you can manage *this*!"

To net this out for you, *just because you CAN do something, and it comes to you relatively easily, does not signify you should or must do it.*

The *Tao Te Ching* is an ancient book of Chinese wisdom, attributed to the philosopher Lao Tzu. It asks, "Can you wait until your mud settles?" to see what you should do?

WHY TRY is in tune with this question. With patience, you can wait your way to seeing what might be right for you.

I've noticed another interesting connection between doing the right things and natural aptitude. Experts do things fast.

My best haircuts consume very little time when they are done by deft stylists. Chatty Cathys and Clarences that schmooze and cut are typically less capable.

My wife, who has classical training, is a very fast painter. She has a vision, and within minutes it appears completed on the canvas.

But wouldn't it be even better if she dedicated more time to its completion?

Heck, no. It would be worse.

But to sell her paintings at a high price, she shouldn't let it be known she is fast. There is value imputed to works that take a long time to complete.

That's the work ethic intruding inappropriately—again.

You see, the key is the result in hand, the product that you create. If you're producing something beautiful or creative, what difference does it make if you accomplished the outcome in one minute or in ten years?

When I was a four-year-old, I recall creating crayoned drawings for my dad, along with my sister. For some reason, he decided to reward us with a few pennies.

That's when art became interesting to me!

My sister carefully rendered her pieces, making beautifully balanced compositions and clearly discernable representations of trees and grass and squirrels, all color-coded.

I scribbled quickly, churning out piece after piece without much respect for detail. Before long, because of my sheer output, I started earning more pennies than she did.

This was not quite an equitable outcome in the sense that she labored longer and harder than me. But from my view, and the way the game was set up, as I saw it, art was art. If I spun out more landscapes and more incomprehensible abstractions than she did, live with it. I cashed in!

Speaking of artists, Picasso was incredibly prolific; so were many of his contemporaries, such as Erté, Miró, and Dali. Legend has it that at one point Sears stores sold Picassos!

One thing about being prolific is that you can't be a perfectionist, sweating the outcomes. If Picasso cared too much about the quality of his objects, he wouldn't be able to make so many of them.

He didn't *try* to produce his pieces in the way an utter amateur is forced to try. For Picasso, the play instinct blended with his energy and focus, resulting in an amazing cornucopia of paintings, drawings, sculptures, and artifacts such as vases and other household items.

Picasso's fame is correlated with the vast number of objects he left behind. The more people were exposed to him, the more popular he became, and the more collectible as well. In economic terms, supply created demand, not the other way around, as many people think market magic happens.

I want to straighten out an inevitable misconception and I think the Picasso example helps. When I ask, WHY TRY? it seems that I am implicitly endorsing laziness and sloth, one of the seven deadly sins.

But there is an assumption behind that inference. The assumption is that without a lot of effort nothing will get done.

That's out of whack. I believe the most inventive people are the ones that are creatively lazy. They want to get more outputs from fewer inputs, because that will save time and permit them to engage in other activities.

For example, I wash my own car. It takes me ten minutes to do, and I do it to my satisfaction. I get rid of more grime in less time!

But get this. My alternative is driving to a commercial car wash. That takes at least ten minutes each way, expending gas and money. Plus, I may have to wait in line, wasting more of my time.

I'm too lazy to take my car to a professional car wash, but it works out better. I schedule the job for exactly the time when I want to do it, not worrying about traffic or bundling it in with other errands.

Laziness is a goad to right activity. The right thing to do is to wash the car myself, and I even get some exercise by doing it.

We should all be seeking the highest and best uses of our time. These are not always activities that bring the most money, but they could be.

If my concern were primarily financial, I would earn more money as an attorney than as an author. But because professional satisfaction is a higher value for me, I write.

In the greater goal of living what I consider to be the good life, authoring is a cool thing to do. Time flies for me when I'm at the keyboard.

As an attorney, I'd constantly be looking at the clock, because I'd be paid that way, based on billable hours. That's no way to get into the zone.

The zone is a mental state of effortlessness. Ballplayers enter it, and when they do, their results are often incredible. Pitchers throw no-hitters and perfect games and can do no wrong. It's as if the universe choreographs their success at such times, and everything simply works out flawlessly.

Artists and others enter the zone too and report similar results.

Mihaly Csikszentmihalyi is a professor at Claremont Graduate University and the author of a very influential book titled *Flow: The Psychology of Optimal Experience.*

His thesis is that people are happiest when they are immersed in what they are doing, in the process.

This is often called *being in the zone* or *in the groove.* Folks in this state feel absorbed and fulfilled.

Almost everyone seeks experiences of flow, because they are so intrinsically rewarding. You might say that we do them mostly for themselves, not necessarily for other outcomes.

One airline executive joked to me about working at his company. "If I didn't work here, I'd pay to watch!" That's how much fun he had between the hours of 8 and 5.

An employee of mine at Time-Life said something similar. "I could make more money somewhere else," he said. "But it wouldn't be nearly as much fun."

To me NOT TRYING is a pathway to the zone, to a flowing experience, and to great personal satisfaction. If you are grimacing, grinding your teeth, sweating every single detail of a task, and especially if you are worrying about the results of your exertions, you are in an antiflow state.

I believe that in every occupation there are practitioners who are in the flow and others who are hopelessly out of it. You see this everywhere. Certain servers in restaurants are really in their element, happy to be dancing from table to table, joyfully doing the most mundane things, even cleaning up after patrons.

Others are totally out of place, misfits, unhappy to serve, forgetful, and really not there at all. In an ideal world, we would all be working in those places and at those careers that enable us to have flow experiences.

Think about some of the most skilled people on the planet: brain surgeons. Their work is delicate and precise. But it isn't overwhelming. On the contrary, it is manageable and, I'm sure, very rewarding.

Their skills, training, and predispositions are all aligned, resulting in generally happy professionals who are great at what they do, and we can be very thankful for that.

The idea of alignment begs for elaboration. Back to Peter Drucker we go. He mentioned something that stuck with me. Speaking about successful companies and various functionaries in them, he said: "If we do a good enough job of marketing, selling becomes unnecessary."

Selling becomes unnecessary. This is an interesting thought, because it runs contrary to some notions I grew up with in my career, notably that there will always be a need for salespeople.

Drucker is saying the opposite: they're not needed if marketing is good enough. Let me clue you in about what he meant.

In his view, marketing is developing a customer. We start with the unmet or underserved needs of a potential customer we'd like to serve. And we build our product or service around what we think they're willing to buy, how they're willing to buy it, when they are willing to buy it, and how it needs to be packaged and financed to get them to buy it as effortlessly as possible.

If this "better mousetrap" is truly better and we let them know it exists in an effective way, then, yes, as the adage says, they'll beat a path to our door to buy it.

In that case, there is no role for salespeople, for persuaders or influencers, because customers persuade themselves once they are presented with a solution to their problem.

Selling comes into the picture when the fit isn't perfect between product or service and customer. Then we need that salesperson to take the shoehorn and wriggle the customer's foot into the shoe. In that case, the shoe won't sell itself.

I'm using this example of selling and its relationship to marketing because it demonstrates the relationship between NOT TRYING and achieving optimal results in most areas of life, both personal and professional.

The more the seller has to sweat to get the shoe to fit, the harder that shoe will be on the customer's foot. The same applies to any job that you might do.

If you have to force yourself into showing up for each shift, there is something dramatically wrong with that job, at least for you. It doesn't fit. It's not the right shoe for you.

We have an obesity crisis in the United States. One-third of adults are grossly overweight. There are two approaches to solving this problem.

One is to change our definition of obesity. Instead of using the BMI, the Body Mass Index, we might come up with a different metric. While this sounds ridiculous, there's some merit in it.

As I've said, I believe most stats that are "one-and-only" measures of something are usually wrong. Your FICO score doesn't tell the entire story of your credit-worthiness, for example. Sure, there is some correlation, but not always.

For example, you need a decent FICO to lease an apartment or a house. But this score may not be at all predictive of how you'll pay your landlord. Housing may be your number-one priority, so you could be in arrears with your credit cards and student loans, yet faithfully pay your rent on time.

Yet a sinking FICO could sink your chances of finding good housing for yourself and for your family.

I'm an athlete with considerable muscle on my frame. And I eat well, avoiding a lot of junk food. Yet my BMI looks bloated. If you looked only at that and you never looked at me or tracked my jogging or karate regimens, you'd be clueless about the healthy me that is buried beneath that one-and-only statistic.

OK, let's get back to obesity. There are folks that have weight problems, which are, in part, fairly measured by BMI. How do we help them to help themselves?

We need to change our thinking about their situation and suddenly start NOT TRYING so hard to get them to conform to a skinnier ideal. I believe they *think* they are hopelessly obese; therefore they behave as if they are, and eat that way.

They stress about their fat, which makes them seek relief, which they obtain temporarily through more eating. I say they should stop trying so hard to adjust their weight.

How do you do that? Focus on something else, like exercise.

Let me give you a personal example. Recently I started jogging at the beach almost daily. It started with a few steps, and that became a quarter mile, which morphed into a mile and more.

I'm doing a comfortable amount while my family swims and boogie-boards. Then we all do some karate together.

This is a fun routine. While I'm jogging, I'm smelling the ocean, watching others' recreation, and spacing out—sometimes casually problem-solving.

It's all good, and then it's done. Incidentally, as I have taken up this happy habit, I've been eating better. Smaller portions, mostly healthy foods, some donuts (yes, that's right: donuts!). Juices and water have replaced heavier beverages.

The amazing thing is I'm fitting into jeans and shirts that I haven't worn in years. My wife is noticing my changing form, although she's more obsessed with it than I am.

Given the WHY TRY? approach I'm taking to life, getting serious about fitness is exactly what I *don't* want to do!

That's a trap, as all obsessions are. This diet or fitness "plan" wasn't planned. Without really caring, I started showing results. If I try for six-pack abs next, I'll stress out and probably ruin everything.

Above all, I DON'T HAVE A GOAL AND I DO NOT WANT ONE!

The minute all of this fitness stuff turns into hard work is the minute I introduce resistance to carrying it on.

Let me say this another way. There is something called *maximizing*. It is trying to get as much of something as you can. King Midas and gold come to mind. He was so obsessed with it that his curse was to turn everything he touched into that substance.

Do you know who maximizes when it comes to weight loss? Bulimics and anorexics maximize until they disappear and die. I don't want that and neither do you, no matter how good we may look in clothes!

We want to optimize, which is getting the *right* amount of results. When Aristotle spoke of the Golden Mean—the amount of something that is neither excessive on the one hand nor deficient on the other—he was characterizing what I'm getting at here.

Optimal anything equals the right amount. And this level of result is best achieved, I believe, by NOT TRY-ING. I am experiencing this at this very moment with diet, exercise, and weight loss. I'm not starving by any means, and I'm sleeping well. My stress level has also diminished.

Let me observe something. When I look out of my home-office window, I see joggers running next to the water, on a path that overlooks a boat channel. Lots of them carry water bottles, which I think is stupid. They aren't running marathons, and they're not jogging in the desert. I believe they are simply making exercise more difficult.

I don't want to hold anything in my hands when I'm running. Holding on to a bottle requires me to try too hard, and it repels flow, which is one of the rewards I get from this activity.

Running and carrying a bottle at the same time is suboptimal. You wouldn't jog with an extra layer of clothing, so why weigh yourself down with foreign objects that have nothing to do with the activity at hand?

Losing weight, exercising, and getting into shape should be easy and comfortable to do. They should be as effortless as possible, and when they are, they are most enjoyable.

We suboptimize the minute we transform these things into *work*, as we do the second we label our activity *working out*. Likewise, what's this thing we call "watching my weight"? Do we run the risk of having it run off when we're not looking?

Here we are, back at this ruinous work ethic. If something is to be respectable and worthwhile in our society, it needs to be an offshoot of hard labor.

That's nuts, folks!

But aren't there people that don't do well at something right away, but catch on later? There are late bloomers, aren't there?

There are, just as there are exceptions to every rule. For instance, I had a person attend one of my public seminars. She expressed interest in having me do some training at her company's site in Stockton, California.

That's pretty typical. Someone is exposed to my ideas and wants help in applying them back at the ranch. But in her case, I followed up to no avail, and then, contrary to my better instincts, I kept in touch to see if she was ready.

At last I got the call, and we did a successful training program. Her last words to me as I walked to my rental car were, "Thanks for your persistence!" She realized she was a tough sale, but she was a grateful client.

Of course I followed up with her later in the hope I could "persist my way" to another deal. That didn't happen.

But I had one happy ending, so what's the problem?

I was rewarded for the wrong thing. Long after I should have jettisoned her as a prospect, as my pursuit became increasingly costly and distracting to me, I should have cut her loose.

Her "thanks for your persistence!" line got me to wondering, "Have I been giving up too soon with others?" That second-guessing of my sales instincts induced me to waste even more time with other barely breathing prospects.

In the aggregate, a WHY TRY? outlook would have been far more effective, which was what I was operating from before she praised me for the wrong behavior.

I read a quote from a savvy salesperson who echoed what I'm saying here, albeit differently. He said that when it comes to prospects, "We don't resist, we replace."

Instead of fighting for someone's business, countering objection after objection, his idea is to let the resistant go and simply say, "Next?"

What about the famous adage "If at first you don't succeed, try, try again?" Isn't resistance an invitation to invoke persistence?

That's old-school thinking. It's against Drucker's notion that selling can become unnecessary if, through smart marketing, we align ourselves with the most receptive prospects.

I've more of a mind to suggest: "If at first you don't succeed, try, try something else," or "someone else" for that matter.

In some companies we've used a T-O system, which stands for *turn over*.

If I am not hitting it off with a potential buyer, if there's a personality clash, for instance, I will T-O the deal to an associate who has a different style than mine. And that seller will do the same, using me to replace them when the going gets tough or they get stuck.

It is really amazing to witness the significant number of tough prospects that quickly become happy customers in this manner. WHY TRY? fights against the notion that we can please all the people all the time.

Maybe I can't help Mr. Smith, but my associate can.

The same principle applies to teachers and students. Under my guidance someone may thrive, but they may wilt and wither under my colleague's.

To go back to the main theme of this book, you may feel incapable of dispatching your debts on your own. Recognize this, and reach out for assistance. Someone else may be far better equipped, by virtue of expertise and emotional distance, to deal with your creditors.

Along this line, many of us try without success to change other people's minds or modify their behavior. Let's say your boss is apt to fly off the handle at trifles, and you find his histrionics abusive.

You can try to metacommunicate, which is talking about the way he communicates in order to improve how he communicates. Sometimes that works. But it is more likely that your superior has put out the vibe that says, "Don't criticize me."

What then?

Instead of trying to change your boss (for the better), simply change bosses!

WHY TRY to change people, especially those that are in power and set in their ways?

Resistance is wrong. It is a signal that a smoother way needs to be found. In this and other cases, a path of less resistance is the smarter path to take.

There is an old adage that says, "A tumultuous courtship signals an even more tempestuous relationship to come."

In everyday terms, this means if you think you two are in conflict now, just wait until later! It's going to get much worse.

We need to become more flexible and more experimental in forming and pursuing relationships, both personal and professional. "I'm not for everybody, and everybody is not for me" is a much better maxim then "I can get along with anybody!"

Chipper and bright as the latter is, it is hopelessly unrealistic. It's just not true. Some people are so disturbed or so different in their values and methods that we cannot get along with them without compromising ourselves or jeopardizing our well-being.

Recognize the friction and retreat!

In my martial-arts training I was taught how to sense hostility quietly rising up in others well before they were aware of their own disturbances. Typically, their body bubbles expand in the way flustered birds fluff-up their feathers, signaling they require more space.

Resistance is futile. Let them have as much room as they need. In fact, if you can, leave the scene well before all heck breaks loose.

This sixth sense for rising danger has served me well. It is actually something I use when I'm driving. Often I can sense when a car will appear out of nowhere and accelerate into my lane or tailgate me. Or I can detect when someone will be making a sudden lane change into my space, enabling me to slow down NOW before it occurs.

The other day I sensed a crazy driver and purposely let him pass me. He slowed and stared at me as he passed, though I didn't turn my head to stare back. Then he did the oddest thing.

He turned his wheels sharply to the right and ran headlong onto and up the curb two lanes away, where his vehicle stalled.

My wife was with me and witnessed the whole sequence. We both blurted out, "He's crazy!" and I'm sure he was.

Had I resisted the guy by staring back or by not letting him pass me, who knows what could have occurred? He could easily have plowed into me instead of directing his anger to that curb.

The moral is that these cues are available to us if we tune into them. Friction is ever-present. The potential for conflict, especially needless and pointless conflict, is everywhere.

WHY TRY to fight it? One of the greatest warriors of all time, the samurai Miyamoto Musashi, said it is better to avoid a fight than to be victorious in a hundred battles.

This is a very hard lesson to learn, particularly if you fancy yourself a fighter—someone who believes that walking away from adversity brands you as weak or incapable.

But we should realize that fighting produces two losers, even if nominally you win. You're bruised or injured, your tranquility is smashed, and residual hostilities can be even worse and more distracting than the original clash, because losers and their families often seek vengeance.

"When is a fight finished?" is frequently a topic of discussion in martial-arts schools. The uncomfortable realization is "Never." We relive it, cycling it through our minds, glorifying our wins, and punishing our opponents and ourselves for our losses.

Imagine a sporting event where there are no laurels awarded to the winner or consolation prizes to the loser. But there is a big, shiny trophy presented to those that choose not to compete.

That would be weird, right? But the true win in life goes to those that can figure out how to avoid a fight.

I recall having a business conflict with a firm in Hawaii that breached a contract. I sought out the counsel of my attorney, whom I had used to establish my corporation. He listened carefully to what I had to say and to my desire to sue that organization. Then he said, very quietly, "It's not worth it."

He lectured me about how much added money I would waste in litigation and in travel to prosecute the case. He concluded the game wasn't worth the candle, even though he himself would earn fees if I charged ahead. "It's better to let this one go and turn your attention to other things," he counseled.

Frankly, I savaged him in my mind. I told myself he was wimping out. He just didn't have the fire in the belly to wage an effective fight; maybe he was just too old to care or to try.

Reluctantly, I did as he said. A few years later, I enrolled in law school and I learned he was right all along. What I interpreted as timidity was really wisdom. I would have wasted money and time in that battle, and victory at the end was by no means 100% assured.

Officially, I could have won a judgment against that firm, but then I would have to collect on that judgment. They could appeal, and it could result in bad publicity for all. When I really knew enough to evaluate that case myself, I saw there really was practically no end to the conflict!

People waste time and energy on distractions of all kinds. Sensationalized news reports get the adrenalin gushing against the world's dictators. Yes, they're bad people. But what can *you* do about them—join the Foreign Legion and attack them?

These are tempests in teapots, emotional disturbances that are created by the new media to addict you to their programming. Similarly, I'm a baseball fan, and my teams' newspapers have blogs where you're invited to comment.

If you're not careful, you can lose gobs of time making points and responding to counterpoints. All of this takes effort, and generally it is effort without tangible reward.

One of my sparring mates in karate marveled at the degrees I completed. "How did you go to law school and find the time to maintain a consulting practice?" he asked.

"I stopped watching TV," I replied quite candidly.

The point is when you learn to NOT TRY to do irrelevant things, you have far more time and energy to RIGHTLY TRY to accomplish other, more vital things.

There is a finite amount of energy, and it is our highest calling to use it efficiently and effectively. The same amount of emotional energy that it takes to do battle daily with a cantankerous spouse can be redirected into starting a business or composing an opera.

Let's apply the WHY TRY? philosophy to the act of communication. In a conversation, if your habit is to try, try, and try, you're probably talking too much. You're a channel hog, seizing all of the attention for yourself.

It is actually easier and more fulfilling to listen more than we're used to doing. Let others express themselves, and, as the adage puts it, they'll start to think you're a gifted conversationalist!

Mozart reportedly said, in music, "The pauses are more important than the notes." I wouldn't know, but I have studied communication and hold a PhD in the subject.

Good communication, communication that makes all parties feel comfortable, is typically shared communication. We listen 50% of the time and speak 50%.

There are exceptions. Power and status differences between the parties may shift the scales in favor of a teacher or to a boss who is ostensibly the local authority on how and when to do things and is permitted to speak more than we do. Yet smart leaders also listen more than they speak, even if by dint of training or experience they have earned the right to hold forth at greater length than we do.

Listening to others makes people feel important. It makes them feel that their ideas are valued.

What should you do in a job interview? Employment sages say it is smart to get the interviewer to talk about herself and about the opportunity instead of relentlessly tooting our own horns.

I know, this can feel uncomfortable at times. Aren't we being too passive, we might wonder? It isn't as if we're bumps on logs, doing nothing.

Some of the greatest performing artists are those that respond well to and take their cues from others. "Acting is reacting" is one way of describing some of the finest dramatic work.

Reacting is another term for listening, nodding, providing eye contact, and sending bodily signals that say "I hear you" and "I wholeheartedly agree" and "I can understand that."

So there is a two-way transmission of energy, because listening is not entirely passive; it's active as well. It takes some exertion to focus not only on what is being said, but on what isn't. We need to read between the lines. But if we're not careful, even our listening can seem too staged, too energetic, and thus contrived and insincere. In other words, we can try too hard, and listening can backfire.

When I was consulting for a computer-software company, multitasking was the rage. The theory was ultrasimple and ultrawrong: why do one thing at a time when you can do two or more?

The concept is to do 100% of something while you're doing 100% of another. In a word, that's impossible. Moreover, it's a prescription for getting acutely stressed out.

I've had two barbers in a row who are no longer my barbers. They took incoming phone calls while I was in the chair being shorn. As you might guess, those were two of the worst haircuts I ever got.

Texting while driving is a crime, and for a good reason. We can't look down and accurately tap tiny keys and keep our eyes on the road at the same time.

On some level, it's understandable that folks want to try. If they could simultaneously accomplish two things, that would be a way to be more productive. But this isn't how most of us operate at optimal levels.

When I'm selling, for instance, I can't handle inbound calls along with outbound calls. I need to complete one to go to another. If I try to juggle, I lose all of the balls I've thrown into the air.

I have to let the inbound go to voice mail, pick up the message, and then call back. Dedicating 100% of my attention to each call is optimal for me. Plus, I get into the flow of each conversation and can dedicate myself to listening completely. This is easier on me, far less stressful, and far more useful than going back and forth.

WHY TRY to multitask when the results will be far worse than doing things sequentially? Perhaps it feels more productive to the practitioner, but that is illusory.

I can't write while listening to my children, who frequently pop into my office to ask a question or to look up tiger photos on my computer. I gruffly grumble, "I'm writing!" and go back to the keyboard. I can't be nice and repel them gently, because that requires so much effort that I'll knock myself out of the zone where I'm writing well and effortlessly. I know how I operate efficiently, and doing a lot of things simultaneously and poorly is not my best methodology.

Now this is important: people that are pushing us to do more, faster, and better than ever are people that want something from us. They want us to toil like robots for them. They're inviting us to become their slaves.

For example, I delivered a professional speech at a convention before a group of 400 participants. I worked on my manuscript over the course of several days, polishing it to a bright sheen.

Because the trade association sponsoring the program wasn't cash-rich, I agreed not only to compose and deliver the keynote speech but also to do a half-hour breakout session afterwards for those that wanted to delve further into my topic.

The speech went well, and at the breakout we had some very interested folks who asked good questions. But at that point I was exhausted. Commuting ninety minutes in Southern California traffic to arrive at the site sixty minutes before my speech, rehearsing its delivery, and then doing a dynamic talk had pretty much tapped out my energy. Doing the breakout after that was the final straw. It was all too much to do in such a short amount of time.

I really should have scheduled a keynote at the middle of the day and a breakout session much later in the afternoon. But that would have required me to have a hotel room, and it would have incurred double the cost. I wanted to be generous and to give as much value as I could, but I should have known I was being pushed out of my comfort zone to do both performances back-to-back.

The moral to the story is threefold: (1) know your optimal style; (2) communicate it to others; and (3) don't allow others to push you out of it.

The key to success in most endeavors, as you can see, is to bother with what counts and to dismiss the rest.

Should you bother to repay? Is it smart to mortgage your future to service a past financial obligation?

You decide.

Let's sum up this section with an analogy. In today's major-league baseball, the biggest prize is winning the World Series. Only one team can do it each year, making the remaining twenty-nine teams technically losers.

But instead of even trying to compete for this greatest of honors, about one-third of MLB teams deliberately decide to trade away their best players to cut their costs. Knowingly, they tank. If they come in last place, they get some rewards that are incredibly good. For one thing, they might qualify to get the first draft pick, a very promising rookie player, the following season. They can rebuild the entire team around this person. Additionally, the biggest loser also gets a cash award. It's called *revenue sharing*.

To net this out for you, many of today's teams have decided it makes more sense to lose than to win, because if they lose, they win!

There are some recent World Series champions, notably the Chicago Cubs and the Houston Astros, that decided to go this route, to their overall long-term benefit.

Having and maintaining great credit is like competing for a world championship. It is enjoyable and a source of pride. But if you are already behind the eight ball, and your credit score is low and you're behind in your payments, and you see there is no way to win, to get out of debt, given your position today, then tanking may be your best play.

In this scenario, why try today and fail, when you can come back tomorrow, try again, and succeed?

Chapter 7

Restoring Your Financial Self-Confidence

Getting deeply into debt and then having to stiff your creditors can be a hard process to handle emotionally.

To address this point, I have outlined some very practical strategies for negotiating your debts to manageable levels and extinguishing them altogether through Chapter 7 bankruptcy.

But there can be a lingering sense of failure. And this can be more costly to you than the sum total of all of your debts.

The stigma of failure needs to be replaced with a restoration of your financial self-worth (FSW). By this I mean that you should endorse these ideas:

1. I deserve good things.
2. I am capable of starting over at any moment I choose.
3. Folks who have been even worse off have recovered financially, and I can too.

Being deeply in debt inflicts financial traumas on us. Every time we're contacted by mail, email, or phone about a past-due bill, there is a little bruise where our financial self-confidence used to be. We're wounded, and we feel diminished.

And it's all too easy to beat up the person in the mirror. In fact, we are commonly our own worst critics. We tell ourselves that because we took on too much debt or spent too much, we're bad people; we can't be trusted with money. We have no "won't power," so we must scissor our credit cards on the spot. We tell ourselves that given a chance, we'll make the same mistake again.

We go overboard in self-derision, and this inflicts a bigger wound than all of the debts in the world could create by themselves.

As Don Miguel Ruiz writes in his self-help book *The Four Agreements* (page 12):

> *How many times do we pay for one mistake? The answer is thousands of times. The human is the only animal on earth that pays a thousand times for the same mistake. The rest of the animals pay once for every mistake. But not us. We have a powerful memory. We make a mistake, we judge ourselves, we find ourselves guilty, and we punish ourselves. If justice exists that was enough. We don't need to do it again. But every time we remember, we judge ourselves again, we are guilty again, and we punish ourselves again, and again, and again. If we have a husband or wife he or she also reminds us of the mistake so we can judge ourselves again, punish*

ourselves again, and find ourselves guilty again. Is this fair?

Of course, the answer is a very loud "no!" It isn't fair.

Because we are not going to repay in dollars, we punish ourselves, exacting a huge, ongoing repayment in guilt and self-downing. This is unnecessary. Worse, it is unwise, and it will delay your overall recovery from the financial mistakes you believe you committed.

We perceive our actions against a backdrop of morality instead of seeing what happened as a result of economic dynamics. This is a distortion of the facts.

The simple truth is that we were offered too much credit given our financial means to handle it.

Of course, no one but us responded to those mailers and online ads for credit cards touting the fact we were "preapproved." We completed the all-so-simple applications. And no one put a gun to our heads to shop until we dropped or until we were over our limits.

In other cases, we have no choice but to take on debt. If you have an urgent medical condition and you have to go to a hospital's emergency room without health insurance coverage for the event, you'll be billed an exorbitant amount.

I went in on one occasion with what turned out to be a kidney stone. Some say the pain is equivalent to giving birth. I can tell you, it defies description.

An MRI was taken, showing the stone, and I was given some painkillers. After a few hours, the stone passed through my body with my urine.

The bill for that episode, without surgery, was over $18,000!

Many people face bankruptcy because they simply cannot pay their medical bills. Certainly doctors, hospitals, and their supporting staff should be compensated. But health-care costs are excessive and out of control measured against world standards.

Who can blame you for seeking medical help, getting it, and not being able to afford the bill when it comes due?

Apart from taking on involuntary medical debts, we need to appreciate that it takes two to tango.

You are in the hole not only because of wrongful spending, but because of wrongful lending!

They should have known better than to open all of those credit lines to you. And they did. As I said earlier, banks and other lenders know they're going to sustain a certain amount of loss. This projection is built into their models, so they may not know that *you* specifically will drown at the end of the fire hose of credit that they are aiming in your direction. But they know that, of those folks with similar incomes, liabilities, types of jobs, living quarters, and communities, X number will meet their financial demise.

Lenders giddily took the risk to get the reward in the form of exorbitant interest rates, which they are able to charge. And they in turn borrowed at supercheap interest rates from their depositors and from the Federal Reserve Board.

And what happens when banks miscalculate and collectively sustain trillions of dollars of losses? The government bails them out, which is exactly what happened in 2009 and beyond during the Great Recession.

Banks don't feel guilt and remorse, as individuals like you do. It's all business to them: making good loans and not so good loans. They're getting paid back as much and as often as they are by making you feel guilty about your obligations. Perceive your nonpayment as going back on your word, or as the equivalent of a criminal act, and they can manipulate you forever.

Baseball great Yogi Berra was famous for his one-liners and crazy wisdom. When he couldn't seem to buy a base hit, he was asked about his slump.

"Slump, I ain't in no slump," he replied. "I just ain't hitting."

He was asked if he blamed himself for not hitting.

He replied: "I never blame myself when I'm not hitting. I just blame the bat, and if it keeps up, I change bats. After all, if I know it isn't my fault that I'm not hitting, how can I get mad at myself?"

I suggest that you apply the same insight to your financial situation. Why blame yourself? What good does it do to approach your next at-bat with self-downing?

How does seeing yourself as blameworthy help with anything?

It is exactly the opposite perception that can dig you out of the hole, helping you to end your slump.

You need to feel confident that you are financially capable. The difficulty you are experiencing had a beginning, and you may be in the middle of it. But it will come to an end. You'll be able to pick up another bat and stride confidently into the batter's box.

That is, if you don't debilitate yourself in the mean-time.

I suggest you start with this affirmation:

I deserve all good things!

Supremely self-confident people act on this premise. They don't blame themselves or imprison themselves in an emotional pit.

University of Pennsylvania psychologist Martin Se-ligman says there are three hallmarks of optimistic peo-ple. They don't tell themselves bad times are (1) personal, (2) pervasive, or (3) permanent.

His model can help us to understand Yogi's wisdom and the functioning of supremely confident people.

For Yogi, hitting is about hitting. It's not personal, and it's not about his essence, or his goodness or badness.

To paraphrase philosopher René Descartes, who fa-mously said, "I think, therefore I am," Yogi doesn't say, "I hit, therefore, I am." He exists independently of his performances. His goodness and badness are not condi-tioned upon how well he's hitting.

You are far more than the sum of your debts.

In fact, once you have stumbled, you have great up-side potential!

You can read up on numerous people that have earned and lost fortunes and then earned them back again.

Reread that sentence, please.

They (1) earned fortunes, (2) lost them, and (3) earned them back again.

This sounds like easy-come, easy-go, doesn't it? On one level it is exactly that way.

Fortune earners tell themselves that if they did, it once they can do it again. Their bad fortune isn't permanent, nor is their good fortune. What is a constant is their supreme self-confidence that they can rise to the occasion after getting knocked down.

Fortunes aren't permanent, and we will recall that this is one of the prongs of analysis Professor Seligman uses in his model of optimists. His third prong says optimists don't say things are pervasive. During the recession that deepened during 2008, trillions of dollars of stock-market wealth disappeared, including some of my assets. On an objective level, there was an enormous slowdown in economic activity. Real estate lost 50% of its value, seemingly overnight. Doom was near.

But even in those times when millions were losing their fortunes some people were building theirs. Billionaire Warren Buffett infused about $5 billion into General Electric stock, one of my losers.

I bought it starting at $28 a share. It had plummeted so low that Buffett observed that a share of stock equaled the cost of a single light bulb that one of GE's divisions produced. How could a company that produced it *not* be a bargain?

GE bounced back to the $28 level (although recently it has experienced a downdraft in valuation).

During the worst times smart people who keep an even keel know that nothing is completely pervasive. Yes, bad times hit just about every sector of the economy, but prudent people see and seize opportunities. They realize the economy is still productive, albeit at a recessionary level.

They blame their bats and not themselves. They see daylight through the darkness, and they know bad times aren't permanent. They are cyclical.

Yogi also famously said, "In baseball you don't know nothin'." This is not just a commentary about baseball. It pertains to almost every endeavor.

Yogi means that everything resets. Life seems like an uninterrupted stream, but it isn't. Suns rise and set. There are certain rhythms and predictable ebbs and flows, but there are also deviations from the norm.

On a sunny October day in 1989, a mighty earthquake stopped the World Series in Oakland, California. The Bay Bridge collapsed, and a huge amount of damage was done. A rain delay or postponement—well, that could be expected. But an earthquake of that magnitude? Forget about it!

Within days, the same Warren Buffett that capitalized on GE's stock meltdown underwrote $2 billion worth of earthquake insurance spanning the next twenty-four months after the Loma Prieta temblor.

Had another big one hit, he'd have taken a huge loss. But he bet that the quake was an oddity, and he won $2 billion.

Buffett is a supremely confident person. He rode in on his white horse to support GE and to restore peace and quiet to Northern California.

Otherwise there could have been a stampede for the exits. Real-estate prices may have plunged, companies could have relocated, and life would have been very different. Some of Buffett's other enterprises could have suffered deep losses or have gone bust.

Jeff Gluck, then a Little League-aged kid who attended that canceled World Series game with his mom, would see his life change nonetheless. She was so spooked by the event that she insisted that her family leave the Bay Area and move to Colorado.

Had this sequence of events not been triggered, Gluck doubts he would have gone into sports journalism, never to chronicle what that shaker meant to him and to his family.

There are two principles at work here. One of them is the *ongoing business theory*. This is the idea that businesses won't close their doors tomorrow. They'll carry on one way or another. And this makes accounting and strategic planning possible.

But there are also *black swans*. These are events so unforeseeable that they shake us to our foundations. One of them was 9/11, which changed my business to this day.

Before that attack on the World Trade Center, flying for business was something I did on a weekly basis. When I did a major consulting program for a Houston-based firm, I flew in and out almost every week for two years.

I was on a similar schedule with a Florida-based insurance company, checking into and out of the same hotel weekly. In fact, this drill was down so pat that I left five suits to be dry-cleaned every Friday so I would have them for my late Sunday evening return.

Then 9/11 struck. I was there in Fort Myers, getting ready for a training class when we got the news. Breaking for lunch, I went back to the hotel's restaurant and was transfixed in the sports bar by the sight of the Trade Center buildings on fire, and then collapsing, in real time.

My return flight was scheduled for that Friday, on a Boeing 777 from Miami to Los Angeles. It was the first plane allowed off the ground during the rest of that week.

We boarded and then we unboarded. The tension was palpable. A flight attendant told me I was the last line of defense next to the cockpit, sitting where I was in first class.

I would return to Florida keeping as much as possible to the schedule we had fashioned, calling for me to do a number of additional seminars throughout the state.

But something dramatic had changed. I couldn't rely on air travel the way I had before to ferry me efficiently and on time to and from assignments. And my clients were suddenly concerned about my safety and the reliability of our schedules.

It wouldn't be long before I decided the tightened security measures and fewer on-time flights were too costly in regard to time and too much of a hassle. Around June 2003, I decided to put my travel bags in the closet for good. My consulting practice reverted to a more primitive state, no pun intended. I would do California programs requiring a one-hour flight or a several-hour drive, but no longer would I hurl myself across the country for extended programs.

The window for maintaining a full business wardrobe 2500 miles away was closed. After 9/11, the Internet became the travel substitute, and a dark age descended on live person-to-person long-distance training.

Black-swan events can change practically all we think we know about the ongoing nature of our businesses. Yogi is right: "we don't know nothin'" when it comes to interruptions of this magnitude.

KNOWING we don't know is the important takeaway here.

Supremely confident people DO know their strengths, and they lead with them. Baseball legend Ted Williams had this key piece of advice to give to fellow players:

"Get a good pitch to hit."

This means don't swing at what you can't hit. If you are a pull hitter and pitchers are throwing on the outside corner, let those pitches pass you by. You won't put your power swing on them, because you won't be able to pull them to the customary field.

Either that or learn to hit to the opposite field. This is also known as *going with the pitch*. If it is thrown on the outside corner, don't try to pull it. Hit it where it is instead of where you want it to be.

This adjustment is easier said than done. When pitches are "in your wheelhouse," meaning they are aimed at your swing's strengths, you have the best chances of reaching base safely or stroking a multiple-base hot or home run.

Supremely confident people know their strengths and their weaknesses, and they (1) either accept them and resist doing what they are not naturally strong at doing, or (2) they make adjustments to their swing.

The greatest hitters, including Tony Gwinn, were keen students of the game. They'd study pitchers and remember patterns of various at-bats against them. And they'd fluidly adjust from pitch to pitch when they were in the batter's box. Again, this is a rare ability, reserved to Hall of Fame players.

There are exceptions. Hall of Fame inductee Vladimir Guerrero was famous for hitting "bad balls" well. So a pitcher couldn't safely find or exploit Guerrero's weaknesses, because he wasn't constrained by set hitting habits.

As I've said, some prominent people believe that working on your weaknesses is foolish and doomed to failure. Peter Drucker said this repeatedly.

It is no accident that many supremely confident people didn't achieve well in school. They intuitively realized they were hopeless in certain areas, or in the formal scholastic system.

And they went with their strengths.

Bill Gates, one of the geniuses behind Microsoft and the rapid expansion of PCs around the globe, dropped out of Harvard. I'm sure it wasn't because he couldn't pass his classes or finish on time. He had something better to do! Developing a computer language was more critical for him (and for the world, may I say) than acing political science or going out for the rowing team.

Gates knew his strengths, and above all, he sensed what he was to undertake would change the world.

There might have been an aunt or grandparent in his family who lamented, "Too bad he dropped out of Harvard! What a pity!" But that observation is exactly the point.

Go back to Drucker's Mozart analogy: Mozart's math was Gates's Harvard degree. Relative to their areas of genius, it would have been completely foolish to have insisted that they do everything well, especially simultaneously.

Yet this is the expectation of schools and of the students they are educating. In more than one book, Drucker says that the effective executive follows this commandment: KNOW THY STRENGTHS.

This invocation applies to all of us. It is a major operating principle in the careers and lives of supremely confident people.

By the way, I believe this is one of the greatest benefits of a broad, general education. By studying multiple topics, we can learn what suits us, and what doesn't. Our strengths can become apparent to us.

The key is to jettison what isn't a good match, not to pine about it or to agonize in persevering for perseverance's sake.

Seen this way, formal education is a chance to reveal weaknesses, not in order to fix them, but to minimize their future importance.

Knowing you hate spinach is a valuable data point at a buffet. You won't put it on your plate, and you'll make room for tastier and equally or even more nutritious fare.

The parent or schoolteacher who bemoans the fact you hate spinach and gets you to think that this is a fault is wasting everybody's time and energy.

Ultimately, knowing your strengths will lead to specialization. There's nothing wrong with this, though it may make you somewhat boring at social gatherings.

In a very good book, author Srully Blotnick studied people who prospered over a twenty-year period. His title is a tip-off to what he found:

Getting Rich Your Own Way.

He examined all sorts of factors with which folks in this study started. Some were high-school grads; others had college degrees and advanced credentials. They went into disparate fields. No matter what their level of formal learning was, or their specific areas of work, the ones that made fortunes had one thing in common.

They got into an area that profoundly interested them, and they stayed in it over the long term.

If they were garment makers, they became fascinated with making the best items they could. Within time, others discovered their superior skills and quality products, and slowly fortunes were earned.

Typically these winners invested their funds in other areas, such as stocks and real estate, and most of them had no idea of their own financial worth. By contrast, those that started out simply wanting to make money weren't nearly as successful as those that fell in love with their work and stayed with it.

What we like to do usually reflects our strengths. But one of the quirks in this is the fact that our strengths are usually invisible to us because they come so naturally.

And in Western societies, informed as we are by the work ethic, we tend to disrespect what comes to us easily, while saving our esteem for difficult challenges.

When I was nineteen and in my freshman year of college, I took a feature-writing class in the journalism department. One of our textbooks was *Writer's Digest*, which lists publishers and their requirements for submitting pieces to them.

I saw a few poetry journals, and on a lark I quickly wrote two pieces of verse and sent them off. I had so many things on my plate that I forgot about these submissions entirely and figured they'd come to nothing. Besides, our teacher had urged us to steel ourselves for the innumerable rejections we could expect to see if we decided to publish.

But within three or four months I was surprised to learn my two poems were being published.

Instead of thinking, "Wow, I have some talent here!" I talked myself out of seeing myself as a poet. "That was way too easy!" I thought. And then I said that anything as easy as publishing poems had to be without much merit.

Initial success is a good sign. You might actually be a natural at something.

Working my way through college and grad school, I sold ballpoint pens part-time for a national office-supply firm. (Actor Johnny Depp reportedly did this too before his career took off.) I sold about three hours a day, three or four days a week, between teaching and taking classes. I went on to train thousands and to author several best-selling books in the field.

Easy initial success can signify that you too are a natural at something. That's like seeing a buy signal on a stock. You should invest more into that activity, as a general rule.

Poetry didn't pay as much as selling, so it is pretty obvious why I pursued the latter and not the former. Indeed that is one of the distractions that supremely confident people face: They might be too good, too fast, at too many things.

Peter Drucker was fond of saying, "If the gods want to destroy you, first they'll give you forty years of success!" He might have added, "and they'll make you good at forty different things."

There are occasional geniuses at many things. Leonardo da Vinci comes to mind.

In business, Elon Musk, who has successfully started a major solar-energy company, Tesla motors, and SpaceX, the first firm to reuse rockets, might also qualify as one of these folks that seem to ooze excellence in every direction. But they are exceedingly rare. It is more common to find that you excel at one thing, or possibly two. The smart thing is to see these strengths as strengths and not as mere knacks or trifles.

Then you should advance headlong into exploiting them. You'll realize multiple wins. Then these successes can be carried over into a generalized sense of self-confidence.

The reason we have discussed supremely confident people is to point out that your financial future is in your hands. Your apparent failure to manage debt is temporary.

It isn't personal, either. It happens to millions of people. And you can press on from here to realize astonishing financial success.

And your mishaps aren't pervasive. You can change your tactics, your environment, and your income to make any current failures things of the past.

You can do it NOW, without anyone else's permission.

You've had some hard times financially. It is all too easy to overgeneralize, to tell yourself they are personal, pervasive, and permanent.

Instead, emulate supremely confident people. Realize these things happen, even to the most successful and famous people.

You can hit the reset button and restore your financial self-confidence.

Do it now!

Afterword

I hope this book has opened your eyes to the options you have for resolving your debts.

As you have seen, there are two aspects to getting a handle on your obligations: technical and emotional.

I've shared some specific techniques for resolving your credit-card debts, back taxes, and student-loan commitments. You've now been exposed to different negotiation postures and principles.

I've also pointed out some additional resources you can consult, including Department of Education and IRS Internet sites.

If you feel overwhelmed about taking the next step or about filling in the paperwork improperly, or if you need a little help in deciding what path to take at this point in your journey, send me a note. I do some coaching and counseling, and I also know some other sources that can assist you.

In the meantime, I wish you the best of luck and know you deserve the best!

Gary S. Goodman PhD, JD, MBA
(818) 970-GARY (4279)
gary@drgarygoodman.com
drgaryscottgoodman@yahoo.com
gary@customersatisfaction.com
gary@negotiationschool.com

Index

Printed in the USA
CPSIA information can be obtained
at www.ICGtesting.com
JSHW012031140824
68134JS00033B/2995